T0355725

Without Proof or Evidence

We face perhaps a more serious bankruptcy in the world of spirit; for the concepts have gradually been emasculated, and the words have been made to mean everything and anything.

Kierkegaard

Explaining something means to make it clear in its significance, that it is this and not something else.

Kierkegaard

Without Proof
or Evidence

Essays of O. K. Bouwsma

Edited and introduced by

J. L. Craft and Ronald E. Hustwit

University of Nebraska Press

Lincoln and London

"Anselm's Argument" was originally published in
The Nature of Philosophical Inquiry, ed. Joseph
Bobik (Notre Dame, Ind.: Notre Dame Press,
1970) and is used by permission; "Adventure in
Verification," was originally published in *God
and the Good: Essays in Honor of Henry Stob*, ed.
Clifton J. Orlebeke and Lewis Smedes (Grand
Rapids, Mich.: William B. Eerdmans Publishing,
1975), and is used with permission of the pub-
lisher; the two *Zettel* papers were originally published in *Essays on Kierkegaard and Wittgenstein*,
ed. Richard Bell and Ronald Hustwit (Wooster,
Ohio: College of Wooster Publications, 1978), and
are reprinted by permission of the College of
Wooster; the University of Chicago Press and
Christopher Middleton have kindly granted permission to use the lengthy quotations from Middleton's translations of Nietzsche's letters, which
later appeared in *Selected Letters of Friedrich
Nietzsche*, trans. Christopher Middleton (Chicago:
University of Chicago Press, 1969).

The paper in this book meets the guidelines for
permanence and durability of the Committee on
Production Guidelines for Book Longevity of the
Council on Library Resources

Library of Congress Cataloging in Publication Data

Bouwsma, O. K.
Without proof or evidence.

1. Philosophy – Addresses, essays, lectures.
2. Theology – Addresses, essays, lectures.
I. Craft, J. L. (James Lee), 1947- . II. Hustwit,
Ronald E., 1942- . III. Title.
B29.B68 1984   190   83-10269
ISBN 0-8032-6227-2

Contents

Introduction

Well known as an essayist on Descartes,
Moore, and Wittgenstein, O. K. Bouwsma was
also an equally committed student of Kierkegaard, a devoted reader of Scriptures, and a
lifelong lover of the reformed church. These
sides of Bouwsma, though less well known,
are integrally related to his teaching, writing,
and conception of philosophy. The papers collected here reveal these sides of Bouwsma and,
by complementing previously published papers, give a more complete view of his philosophical thoughts.

Bouwsma's literary estate, now located at
the Humanities Research Center, University
of Texas at Austin, consists of eight boxes of
papers, legal-pad journals, and reproductions
of notes prepared for seminars. One box contains typescripts and mimeograph copies of
papers that he had read at colloquies at various
universities, circulated privately, or written
for special occasions. We gathered the unpublished papers, added several that had already
been published in not-readily-available places,
edited them, and divided the material into two
groups according to a thematic division: those
concerned with religious themes and those
not.

The first of the two resulting volumes, Toward a New Sensibility (Lincoln: University
of Nebraska Press, 1982), contains the philo-

sophical papers on nonreligious themes. Some of those papers exhibit Bouwsma's approach to the problems of philosophy as presented in, say, a particular passage from Descartes or Berkeley, or in a remark by a student or a colleague. Some present Bouwsma's conception of philosophy and its indebtedness to Wittgenstein.

This second volume presented more editorial problems than the first. These problems did not stem from the shape or quality of the manuscripts, but from the nature of their contents. Because the themes, questions, and problems were religious in nature, and because of Bouwsma's attitude towards religion, the editorial questions of how to prepare the reader and present the papers in the proper light proved to be more difficult than with the first volume. Philosophical problems may interest one or not, but religious problems are not merely a matter of interest, inclination, or disposition. Religious problems are problems of how to live, what to believe, what it means to be a human being, where to build one's foundation. Salvation is not a philosophical problem, though philosophical problems may surround the concept of salvation, and it does not enter from the doors of Plato or Descartes or Berkeley or Wittgenstein.

The reader will notice that in *Without Proof or Evidence* Bouwsma weaves through the central topics of Western religion: the rationality of religious belief, the nature of Christianity, the promise of eternal life, the definition of faith, proofs of the existence of God. When he works with the problems of Descartes or Moore or Wittgenstein, surveying the marketplace of language in which we all have commerce, he has the familiarity of an experienced trader. But in his work with the problems of Anselm or Nietzsche or Kierkegaard, in which the Scriptures move between background and foreground, there is another dimension, a concern whether the Scriptures have been properly understood, what such an understanding might be, and how it affects someone who so understands them.

A central theme of these papers is the remarkableness of a book which God has sent to mankind. God is a writer or a consignor of writers, and now there is a book that is a collection of stories, history, songs, poems, parables, laws, eyewitness accounts, teachings, proverbs, prophesies, and letters. What is the reader to do with this book? What is its purpose? How do its various forms of literature and concepts relate to the realization of that purpose? How is one to find out? Bouwsma examines the uses of the concepts in the texts. He is sensitive to the variety of concepts, the power of their linguistic forms to fascinate and bewitch, and their rich relationships to human beings in the stream of life. He has cultivated an ear for detecting differences in the uses of concepts. These differences, once revealed, illuminate, instruct, redirect one's energies, and restate the problems.

An important aspect of detecting differences in the uses of concepts of Scripture is to see the particular texts as containing reminders for orienting one's intelligence when it is confused by the philosophically troublesome concepts of faith, belief, proof, and evidence. The Scriptures provide paradigms of faith in Abraham, Moses, Saint Paul, and others. What does faith look like in these cases? What evidence or proof did these men have for their belief in God? These questions help clarify the concept of faith. Bouwsma suggests that reflection on those cases reveals that *belief* in the religious sense is conceptually connected to *obedience* and not to *evidence* or *proof.* Such a suggestion, which aligns Bouwsma with Kierkegaard, undermines many theories and claims in the philosophy of religion.

In "Faith, Evidence, and Proof" Bouwsma examines the notions of evidence and proof with respect to religious beliefs. What could count as evidence that, for example, God has spoken to Abraham as we read in Genesis? What could count as evidence that Saint Paul was acting under orders from God and was not deluded? When Saint Paul was asked for something like proof, or a defense, at his trial, he told the story of his calling and obedient response. Recalling and retelling the stories of faithful response and drawing attention to details are the equivalent here of arranging conceptual or logical insights in order to disentangle philosophical problems. This notion of "telling a story" plays an important role in Bouwsma's conception of philosophy of religion and can be put to different uses to emphasize a variety of conceptual differences.

In the lecture "The Invisible" Bouwsma remarks, "There is no subject more bewildering and more frustrating than the subject of religion or, as in the present circumstances, than Christianity. And this is because of the role of the Scriptures." The issue is the understanding of the Scriptures, and it is discussed in depth, utilizing what Bouwsma appropriated and adapted from Wittgenstein. What blossoms from the effort is something quite unexpected, a new flowering of religious sensibility, not another interpretation among others. As always, Bouwsma does not fret over understanding in general, but takes particular examples—the first sentence of Genesis, the story of Noah, the eleventh chapter of Hebrews—and cultivates the uses of the concepts in those contexts in order to achieve clarity and orientation. How does one understand

Moses, Noah, and Saint Paul and their faith in the Invisible? What did they say? How did they respond? What is the story of Moses from the reed basket to the promised land? What is the story of Saint Paul from persecutor to apostle? To work those stories out, separating what is significant from what is not, emphasizing the appropriate details, is a contribution to the understanding of the concept of faith.

The paper "Anselm's Argument" treats from another angle the question of proof in religion by examining the Euclidean charm of the ontological argument. Bouwsma works in detail on the relevant passages from Anselm's *Proslogium*, discussing five key sentences in the ontological argument and asking, "How are we to understand what Anselm is doing?" Many have been prepared to prove, reprove, or disprove the ontological argument, but Bouwsma questions what Anselm is doing and for whom he is doing it. By questioning that, Bouwsma is led to search for the biblical contexts in which the concepts, phrases, and expressions Anselm uses have precedence. The search takes him to the Psalms.

How are the concepts of the Psalms, such as "the greatness of God," being used? Are they serving to make claims or assertions? Anselm seems to think so, and Bouwsma undermines that. He works patiently with Anselm's passages and the related Scriptural concepts in order to achieve conceptual clarity and an understanding of what led Anselm to advance his version of the ontological argument. If someone makes an argument, he needs first to provide the prerequisite understanding of the concepts used in the sentences of the argument. This prevents mis understandings, among other things. Such understanding is captured in the natural habitat of the concepts, in this case pursued in the Psalms.

The paper on Kierkegaard considers the nature of Kierkegaard's task, the point of view in his authorship, by treating the expression "the illusion of Christendom" as the critical point in grasping his overall motive. Bouwsma remarks, "Kierkegaard must work out the consistency of the Christian, his life, and his language. How does God enter into the life of a man to challenge him and to promise?" Bouwsma struggles with the expressions of belief in Christianity, such as "I am a Christian," in order to understand how someone could believe himself a Christian and yet not be a Christian. He looks to the Scriptures and their role in the uses of such expressions of belief in order to gain perspective. There are also several intriguing parallels that Bouwsma draws between Wittgenstein and Kierkegaard, in particular, with respect to dissolving illusions.

In "Miss Anscombe on Faith" Bouwsma points out in no uncertain terms that the correct conceptual understanding of the question "What is faith?" shows that it cannot be a calm, cool, collected question that has flown from brain to brain in want of a clean, well-lit definition. It is not a clear question, first; and as a question connected to the religious life, it is one asked from the depths of the soul, brought forth in fear and awe, despair and hope, upsetting intelligence with the promise of the unbelievable. It is not a question for the cleverness of Russell or the wit of Bierce, and Bouwsma turns to Saint Augustine and Dostoevsky for contrast. There is emotional electricity, a highwire current, a tension in religious questions, and that tension can be felt throughout these pages.

The paper "Adventure in Verification" concerns again the themes of evidence, proof, verification, and objectivity with respect to religious beliefs and is written as a story of a man who undertakes the task of verifying a certain religious belief. This method, or approach, of inventing a story, filling out the surroundings with human detail and dust, in order to provide sense for an expression or concept could be called the narrative approach. This narrative approach shows how, if one will free the term "refutation" from its ancient philosophical prison, one might undertake a philosophical "refuting" of the concept of verification with respect to religious beliefs. But notice that Bouwsma does not argue that no one can verify a religious belief, as if one could try but the mountain is just too high for human hearts; instead, he shows that the unraveling of the expressions and circumstances of such a verification produces no use, and no clear use can be invented. There are no procedures for action, no steps to follow the stairway to heaven. But merely saying that has no philosophical punch. The punch comes out in the story and its drama.

The paper on Nietzsche, written as an introduction to a volume of Nietzsche's letters, is full of that tension and high voltage mentioned earlier. Bouwsma tries various ways of getting at the question "What is Nietzsche doing?"—even suggesting at one point that perhaps Nietzsche and God have an understanding and that Nietzsche is following orders. Is Nietzsche a sheep in wolf's clothing? In this paper Bouwsma tries to clarify his thoughts on Nietzsche by comparing him to Ivan Karamazov in Dostoevsky's *The Brothers Karamazov* and using material from his discussions with Yorick Smythies, a student of Wittgenstein, whom Bouwsma met at Oxford. Smythies introduced Bouwsma to Dostoevsky's *Notes from the Underground*, and it was planned that Bouwsma, Smythies, and Wittgenstein would discuss the book; Wittgenstein's illness prevented his participation. Smythies and

Bouwsma went ahead with the discussions, and through them Bouwsma became intrigued with the idea that a person represents himself to others for a motive, in order to create a certain impression. Smythies wrote a paper on that topic titled "Non-logical Falsity," which has not to our knowledge been published, but which Bouwsma circulated. Since Bouwsma is here writing of Nietzsche, the man of his letters especially, the idea of representing oneself for a motive is relevant. This also explains why Bouwsma bypasses the notions of eternal recurrence, the overman, tremendous moments, the will to power. In the paper Bouwsma remarks, "Think of Nietzsche as a storm, thunder and lightning and wind, a natural force, a tornado, ruthless, tearing away at the landscape, spreading ruin."

The papers "Lengthier *Zettel*" and "A Lengthy *Zettel*" echo Wittgenstein's *Zettel* and are, as the names imply, cuttings or scraps that Bouwsma clipped and organized from his philosophical diary. There are many topics in these cuttings interwoven with remarks on Socrates, Freud, Kierkegaard, and Hegel. The questions "Is belief in God rational?" and "How many gods are there?" tie the papers neatly in with the others of the volume and bring out another manifestation of the desire to defend and shore up Christianity with philosophical propositions.

There are scores of variations on a theme in these papers. Among the variations are these: the rationality of religious belief, the role of proof and evidence in religious contexts, the search for definitions of faith, the verification of religious beliefs, the objectivity of the religious life, the nature of religious language, the role of the Scriptures in Christianity. Bouwsma approaches these perplexities not as a distanced, detached critic, unconcerned with the events and persons, their story and drama, but rather as someone seriously, passionately concerned with their significance and the understanding of them. The problems of religion, of Christianity in this case, are the most personal, profound, perplexing problems of life. What could be more personal than the hope of eternal life?

Bouwsma's particular contribution to the issues, as philosophers and theologians of this generation are trying to formulate and solve them, is the insight that underlying all issues of evidence, proof, definition, verification, argumentation, objectivity, and rationality, is the issue of understanding, in these cases, understanding the Scriptures. How is one to understand the Scriptures? Until the many Scriptural concepts and their linguistic forms are put in perspective, there will be no rest from the philosophical demands for evidence, proof, and definition. Such demands in the philosophy of religion are the products of a lack of understanding and hence of clarity. This understanding is the result, not of some general theory, but of work on particular passages, sentences, and expressions of the Scriptures. But such understanding cannot be paraded about the drill field of philosophy and thereby accounted ready and fit for action. It must be engaged in battle, and its skills, techniques, and art were developed in the heat of battle. The battle in this case is against the confusions one develops in trying to formulate a philosophical defense or explanation of religious beliefs. Bouwsma wrote of such battle in his notebooks and describes Wittgenstein's aims in the *Philosophical Investigations* as follows:

The book *Philosophical Investigations* may be described as skirmishing in a continuing warfare against the fascination which the forms of language exert upon us. The warfare is not orderly, and there are no decisive battles as though there were a time when the war was over. Like most of life's problems, this struggle lasts a lifetime and continues from generation to generation. In struggling, Wittgenstein has shown us how to fight. At no point does Wittgenstein say, "Now I have won." In this warfare, the dead rise again to fight. What Wittgenstein does is to describe for us what our warfare is, war aims, and how the fight is to be carried on. Then he goes on to fight. He might have said, "Watch me." And that is certainly what we who read Wittgenstein may do. We learn from him how to fight.

The same may now be said of Bouwsma and this book, and that one may also learn from him "how to fight" for conceptual clarity.

As in the first volume, we have provided a headnote at the beginning of each paper that will date it, give some background of its occasion, and, in some cases, help orient the reader in the direction of the paper. We have provided titles for "Faith, Evidence, and Proof," "An Introduction to Nietzsche's Letters," "Myth and the Language of Scriptures," and "The Biblical Picture of Human Life." All other titles are Bouwsma's. As almost all of these papers were read at university philosophy department colloquia, there were very few grammatical changes and other textual changes that needed to be made. Because of Bouwsma's unique, sometimes Joycean style, we sometimes had to decide between that style and more standard grammar. We chose the former unless we felt a mistake had been made in the grammar. We changed a few sentences that were confusing to follow as written, if several re-readings would not clarify the confusion. Sometimes sentences were deleted if they were peculiar to the particular audience to whom the paper was addressed. A part of one paper and several papers from the Texas collection were omitted because of redundancy. This is explained in the appropriate headnotes. Finally, the reader should note that the order of the papers is not chronological. Rather, they are arranged so that readers not familiar with Bouwsma or philosophy would be brought into the readings by way of more general concerns.

Finally, we would like to acknowledge support from the Bouwsma family, the University of Texas at Austin Humanities Research Center, and the College of Wooster. The latter, through several grants from the Faculty Development Fund, made travel, typing, and manuscript reproductions possible.

Without Proof or Evidence

Faith, Evidence, and Proof

This paper has no title on the typescript, but Bouwsma alludes to one shortly into the text. We have provided a title appropriate to that allusion. It reflects, we believe, themes central not only to this paper but to all the papers in this collection. We do not know where nor on what occasion the paper was read. It was written in 1968.

I am going to begin by quoting from a conversation between characters in *The Brothers Karamazov*. The chapter is entitled "Over the Brandy." As you might guess, there has been some drinking. The characters are a dissolute and despicable father, Fyodor, an intellectual son, Ivan, and a religious and saintly son, Alyosha. The father says, "Speak, all the same, is there a God, or not? Only be serious. I want you to be serious now." He has addressed himself to Ivan.

The conversation now goes on:

"No, there is no God."
"Alyosha, is there a God?"
"There is."
"Ivan, and is there immortality of some sort, just a little, just a tiny bit?"
"There is no immortality, either."
"None at all?"
"None at all."
"There's absolute nothingness, then. Perhaps there is just something? Anything is better than nothing!"
"Absolute nothingness."
"Alyosha, is there immortality?"
"There is."
"God and immortality?"
"God and immortality. In God is immortality."
"H'm! It's more likely Ivan's right. Good Lord, to think what faith, what force of all kinds, man has

lavished for nothing on that dream, and for how many thousands of years. Who is it laughing at man? Ivan! For the last time once for all, is there a God or not? I ask for the last time."

"And for the last time there is not."

"Who is laughing at mankind, Ivan?"

"It must be the devil," said Ivan, smiling.

"And the devil, does he exist?"

"No, there's no devil either."

"It's a pity. Damn it all. What wouldn't I do to the man who first invented God: Hanging on a bitter aspen tree would be too good for him."

"There would have been no civilization, if they hadn't invented God."

"Wouldn't there have been? Without God?"

"No. And there would have been no brandy either. But I must take your brandy away from you, anyway."[1]

It's as though man lived in an enclosure with thick walls and dummy doors. Men pull at and push against the dummy doors—which might also be described as doors for dummies—trying to push open or to pull open, but apart from their illusions that the dummy door has given way just a chink, the dummy door does not open. Men cannot find their way to look out. All the same they cannot get rid of the idea that there is something outside the wall. So they talk about it and talk about it— some say that there is nothing but darkness there, nothing at all. It frightens them. Others say that there is indeed something there, that the door opened just a chink. "I had a glimpse of it. I saw it and it vanished. The door closed." But when they talk about this they discover no agreement. "I saw a dragon." "He saw a beautiful woman with a veil." "I saw a high mountain; and splendid giants lived on that mountain." When they ask other questions, such as "And what has that to do with life in the city, with us, and with our prospects, and what about death?" again there is no agreement. People begin to mistrust the chinks and to say, "They are all dummy doors." They may even have some account of how the dummy doors got there. And they say, "If you keep on pushing at and pulling on a dummy door, the exhaustion and the desperation—as though your push and your pull were your only hope— may soon produce the illusion of chinks and of light coming through." And the people pity one another. But they do not respect one another. To every man his chink, his illusion.

Now, let us return to the conversation I quoted. Presumably the

---

1. Fyodor Dostoevsky, *The Brothers Karamazov*, trans. Constance Garnett (New York: Norton, 1976), p. 122.

father and the two sons are in the enclosure and the walls are thick. They are all aware of the walls. There is now an interest in what is outside the walls. This is what the old man is asking about. His interest is not simple. He may be a bit disturbed by whether there is something outside the wall that he should fear and which might then deter him from drinking more brandy and carrying on as he does. His mocking tone is or may be interpreted as a defense against fear. So he asks, "Is there a God or not?" This is one way of asking, Is there anything outside the wall? We may describe him as a deep trifler. His depth is on the surface and far below he is shallow. But he is also interested in watching Alyosha smart under the lash of Ivan's answer. Ivan answers: "No, there is no God." And who is Ivan? I have already described Ivan as an intellectual. But he is also complex. For one thing, he is not interested in answering his father, whom he regards as a buffoon. On this occasion he humors his father. All the same he is no trifler. He is in dead earnest and, one might say, in the earnestness of death. He has tried every dummy door in the wall and looked out more desperately for a chink than anyone who ever pushed before him. And why? Because life within the enclosure has made him sick. The only thing that sustains him is his own intellectual brilliance, which is at the same time the source of his misery. For with all that brilliance, upon which he then depends, he cannot find the chink he needs. By the time this conversation takes place he has given up. There are no chinks. And if there are no chinks, then Ivan is in despair. In despair of what? I should now mention that Ivan is preoccupied with Christianity. He has been stung with the ethical requirement "Thou shalt love," and he has been at once attracted and repelled by it in the person of Alyosha. Hence when I say that he is in despair it is not of knowing something. He is in despair concerning himself, concerning the contrast between what he is and the requirement. He is damned, since he is without hope that he can ever be anything but what he is. "Ivan is a tomb." "I couldn't even become an insect." As for God, then, who might bring about the change—well, the chink was to provide for that and there is no chink. Chinkless, Ivan spends his life in darkness. Darkness is in the eyes of those who see no light. What light?

Alyosha is no intellectual. I do not mean that he is not bright. I mean rather that he understands his brother well enough, he understands all that I said about the dummy doors and that his brother has pulled at and pushed at those dummy doors. I mean that he has himself not tried to find a way, a chink, to look out beyond that enclosure. You have surely noticed, however, that when the father in that conversation turned to Alyosha and asked, "Alyosha, is there immortality?" Alyosha said, "There is," and when his father went on, "God and immortality?" Aloysha said, "God and immortality. In God is immortality." And Alyosha did not say that he pushed a door open, that he discovered a chink. And the important thing is that this neither worries him nor concerns him. But what then? In such an enclosure as I have described and in which such a conversation may take place there are not only dummy doors which tempt people, but there are also doors, or at least one door, which open only from the outside of that enclosure. And when that door is opened—it is obviously opened only by what is outside the wall and does not even show from inside the enclosure—and one sees what is to be seen, naturally he has no interest in those other doors others try so hard to open. Alyosha may be represented as having stood before such a door. And that explains how it came about that Alyosha could answer as he did. It might be well to notice that no one in this conversation said, "Well, probably" or "Very unlikely." The old man said, "It's more likely Ivan's right," but as I suggested earlier, the old man has an interest in that answer. It keeps the cork out of the brandy bottle. Besides, he would trust Ivan, who had tried the dummy doors, more than one who quite gratuitously saw outside the wall and who said the door opened from the other side.

The conversation with which I introduced this paper represents the situation in which we find ourselves. In any random group of people, were someone to ask the question "Is there a God or not?" there would be at least two answers: "No, there is no God" and "Yes, there is." That they are in the same room together and that they are all extremely intelligent people will not ensure that after they have discussed the matter, they will then have come to an agreement. It was this situation that led me to the suggestion that we are like people who live in an enclosure behind walls, and that the question "Is there a God or not?" is a question about what is behind the wall. This question may be asked idly, as a matter of curiosity—"Oh, is there?"—but it is commonly asked because whether there is something behind the wall, and now depending upon what is behind the wall, may determine how we are to live and what we may expect. Certainly people may be uneasy about this throughout their lives. But how strange it would be if it were the case that everything of importance—"what your sins and miseries are"—should depend upon what is quite beyond us. No wonder, then, that so many of us pound on the walls and like prisoners shake the bars or, as the more learned do, push hard on the dummy doors. Before I go on I want to suggest answers to the question above. There is Ivan's answer: "There is nothing, nothing at all." Another answer is: "There's something but we don't know what." A chink is not a knothole. Last there is Alyosha's answer. And in connection with that answer he has got to say, "The door was opened." And he might have said, "The door walked among us." "Verily, Verily, I say unto you, I am the door of the sheep."

There is one thing connected both with the title of this lecture and the sort of discussion or conversation we noticed. To many of us who are engaged in such conversations, the question that is asked may be embarrassing, not because we cannot readily answer, but because we do not know how to go on. Misunderstandings arise and ensue. And the question itself may be the expression of a misunderstanding. It may be expected, for instance, that Ivan, who says, "No, there is no God," can give a good account of himself. He can give reasons. He can give a recital of horrible cruelties inflicted, not upon people "who have eaten of the apple," but upon small children who have as yet tortured no one. He could say, "No, thank you" to a God who would and does permit such things. Of course, this is a way of saying that he knows nothing about what is on the other side of the wall. It cannot be a God who loves little children. Notice that Ivan in this case discovers certain things that take place in the enclosure, inside the walls, from which to infer what there cannot be outside the enclosure. This situation presents a great temptation to anyone who, like Alyosha, says that there is both God and immortality—not that Alyosha knows either. He too will look about him for whatever he may feel necessary and useful, and of course, he is within the enclosure. Like Ivan, he is a human being who can see only what is within the enclosure. So he is embarrassed without proofs or without evidence. He looks for some fact or facts to serve as evidence— through which to see through the wall. It is these purported facts to which I referred as dummy doors which, when he pushes them, give him the illusion of the chink and light. It is not unusual to hear defenders of the faith speak of Christianity as intellectually respectable, by which they mean that one can give a reason or a proof that is respected also by unbelievers. In this enterprise they are commonly baffled, since they who aim at being intellectually respectable are themselves not without intelligence. Hence their intelligence keeps them uneasy and now they look for help. Where is this evidence to be found? Since I have already referred to the dummy doors, it must be obvious that I do regard the doors as dummy. I might accordingly refer too to the evidence as dummy evidence. A dummy door is not a door. It only looks like a door. A piece of dummy evidence is not evidence. It only looks like, sounds like, evidence. If you push at the dummy door, it does not open. And there is no chink.

II

I want now to return to a more detailed discussion of the enclosure. The enclosure is where we all live, believers and unbelievers alike. If someone were to object, "Ah, but you have forgotten that the Bible is in that enclosure," I should say that I have not forgotten and that I was coming to that. I wanted, especially, to speak of that. We may be sure too that in the background of that conversation I quoted earlier there is the acquaintance with the Scriptures. Accordingly we may understand Fyodor's question in this way: Is the Bible true? And I will now take the liberty of translating this question into "Is the story true?" Before going on I should like to say some things about the Bible.

I have just referred to the Bible as a story. And in accordance with that we may speak of Christianity as something that happened. But it is an utterly fantastic thing that happened. I am emphasizing that Christianity is something that happened and not a theory or an explanation or a set of doctrines in order, at the outset, to make sure of what sort of evidence one might look for were one tempted to look. So too it is not anything that someone discovered, as though one stood behind a tree and then later reported, "I saw it with my own eyes." Naturally, if we say that it is something that happened, then we seem to lay it open to historical investigation. If we said that Moses while tending his flock in the wilderness of Midian saw a burning bush—well, that seems unlikely, but then again, there might have been a burning bush. Surely there have been burning bushes. And if we say that a child was born in Bethlehem and that there was no room in the inn—well, more than one child has been born in Bethlehem, and now and then it happens that there is no room in the inn. That would not have been the first time. But if someone says that God spoke to Moses out of the burning bush and that the child born in Bethlehem was none other than the Lord of life, well, that is something quite different. We all know that the story to which I have now referred is a long, long story and that the happening is a long, long happening. The happening takes place over many centuries, the story is composed of innumerable episodes—a story that is continued in sequels indefinitely. This story may be described either as a story of what I have called the enclosure and "all that therein is" or as the story of what God has done. In the latter case one may also describe the story as a love story. I should like to add that the Christian himself becomes a character in the as-yet-unwritten continuation of the story. He becomes this, however, only as in some way he becomes a believer in that love story. I am adding this, but with misgivings, especially since "believing" in this context may be misleading. Unless, believing in that love story, he sees in it a story about himself and rejoices and is transformed, he does not believe. For to believe is to believe in Him.

Now I want to return to the idea of evidence. Under what conditions can something we know be evidence for something we do not know? I'll suggest: Only in those cases that are analogous to cases in which we know both what corresponds to the evidence in this case and what we come to know by way of that evidence. Consider the story of a murder. If we did not know the pattern of murder, how the facts in a case of murder are connected, what is relevant and what is not relevant, the pattern allowing for innumerable variations, we should not be able to recognize what is evidence, what are clues, and what a reasonable conclusion. A murder is committed, the body is discovered. There are clues, a knife, a bloody shirt, fingerprints. The detectives get busy. The knife and the shirt and the fingerprints—whose are they? The idea is to fill out the details of the story of that murder. We begin with fragments and then elaborate. Capote could write the story of a murder—*In Cold Blood*—because the pattern of murder is familiar. Hence he knew what to look for.

But the divine story is not like that. There may be many reports of murders, many murder stories, many murder mysteries, but there can be but one story of the Creation of the world. I mean by the latter statement that the believer can recognize but one such story as the story. No one is to say that this is the story of Creation because it follows the pattern of all the other such stories. We cannot make any enquiry here concerning the Creation or who it was created the world. Notice that what serves as evidence is always what we know. Otherwise it cannot serve in our defense. We who use the evidence and those who are to be persuaded must agree concerning the evidence, namely, the facts. If now we speak of the Scriptures as a story, a continued story, we can then distinguish in that story always two facets, the human and the divine. We can see this in the story of Abraham. Notice then: "Now Jehovah said unto Abraham, 'Get thee out of thy country, and from thy kindred . . . unto the land that I will show thee: and I will make of thee a great nation, . . . and in thee shall all the families of the earth be blessed.' So Abraham went, and Lot went with him; and Abraham was seventy and five years old. . . ." Part of this story has the texture of the enclosure. "Abraham went." Anyone in Haran in those days who was at all interested might have taken notice. Abraham went and Lot went with him. It might have been in the newspaper. After all, the Bible is a newspaper, the good-news paper. The point about this, however, is that if this were all that was in the newspaper it would not have been the good-news paper. Let me repeat: It all takes place in the enclosure; years later people in Haran might have said: "And that is where Abraham lived." To anyone who might have been interested in the history of the family they could have told some stories. Abraham had been well known there, a prominent settler. They might have known that Abraham had come from Ur of the Chaldees to Haran. And now I might add that Abraham told the people in Haran that Jehovah had spoken to him, though Abraham might have kept it to himself. Supposing, however, that Abraham did tell his neighbors that God had spoken to him, they might also know then that Abraham believed that God had spoken to him and that in leaving Haran he was obeying God. There are some difficulties with this, but for the moment we'll pass them by. But can we now ask: "And did God speak to Abraham and did God promise Abraham that he would make of him a great nation?" We are not to say that since Abraham believed that God called him and that God promised, it must be so or very likely be so. After all, Abraham was a successful man and there must have been many occasions on which he had to be careful, and certainly he would have been careful here. He was a shrewd man. He must have had good reasons, have made an investigation of who this was who was telling him to get up and "go into a land that I will show thee." Abraham may not have relished the idea of journeying into a strange land. And so once again surely Abraham would have asked for guarantees. "How am I to tell?" But the Scriptures say nothing of the sort. The Scriptures say, "And Abraham went," and later, "And Abraham believed." They do not say, "After having taken all the reasonable precautions against being taken in and after making sure that he would be able to give a good account of himself to his friends, he decided to obey the order." They do not say that, after all, Abraham, like other men, had his pride and could not stand it that other men should smile at him, especially other men who read books. But once again we are told: "And Abraham went."

Earlier I distinguished in the Bible and particularly in the story the two elements, the human and the divine. My point in doing that and in discussing the episode in the life of Abraham was to connect the idea of evidence with the human part and to distinguish that from the divine. Of such things as that Abraham went and that Lot went with him, there could be evidence. And of this, that Abraham believed that God spoke to him and promised to make of him a great nation, of this there could also be evidence. But neither we nor Abraham could have evidence that God either spoke to him or did promise him anything; not even Abraham could have evidence of this. In making or insisting on the distinction I do not mean to say that we have any evidence that Abraham did anything. It is obvious, however, that many have believed that there was a man named Abraham and that he did these things. I am interested in emphasizing that the religious belief of Abraham, namely, that God commanded him to go and promised him a future, this belief is of an altogether different order. For this there can be no evidence. I dare scarcely say that we can understand this, I mean, understand what Abraham believed.

If anyone should ask why I discuss just this, my explanation is that the story of Abraham exemplifies the way in which the human and the divine are intertwined in the living of the religious life. It is also the case that in the Scriptures Abraham is the exemplar of faith, "the Father of the faithful," not the exemplar of those who are clever and who can open dummy doors. He is in the world, "he went," but not of the world, "he obeyed God." He is in the enclosure, but his life is directed from what is outside the wall. But how can a man in the enclosure receive orders, directions, promises, etc., from outside the enclosure? Should I say that he listens, presses his ear against the wall? The prayer is: "Incline thine ear." But might not the command be the same: "Incline thine ear." Is it an odd thing that whereas in the Scriptures it is said "no man hath seen God," it is not said "no man hath heard God." There may be something deep in that. Should we say that the heart and conscience can hear, but cannot see? Cannot see what? One can see neither commands, "Go," nor promises, "I will." But the commands and promises can be heard; can one also hear that they are divine requirements and divine promises? Here again is room for belief, for the faith.

Now consider the following passage: "Now Moses was keeping the flock of Jethro, his father-in-law, the priest of Midian: and he led the flock to the back of the wilderness and came to the mountain of God unto Horeb, and the angel of Jehovah appeared unto him in a flame of fire out of the midst of a bush; and he looked and, behold, the bush burned with fire and the bush was not consumed. And Moses said, 'I will turn aside now, and see this great sight, why the bush is not burned.' And when Jehovah saw that he turned aside to see, God called unto him out of the midst of the bush, and said, 'Moses, Moses.' And he said, 'Here am I.' And he said, 'Draw not nigh hither: put off thy shoes from off thy feet, for the place whereon thou standest is holy ground.' Moreover he said, 'I am the God of thy father, the God of Abraham, the God of Isaac and the God of Jacob.' And Moses hid his face; for he was afraid to look upon God." There follows, as you may remember, a long conversation. Towards the end there is this passage: "And Jehovah said unto him: 'Who hath made man's mouth? or who maketh a man dumb or deaf or seeing or blind? is it not I, Jehovah? Now, therefore, go . . . ." After more words we are told: "And Moses went . . ." (Exodus 3–4).

My interest in the passage is once again to draw our attention to the human, the seen, the area in which there could be evidence, and on the other hand, the divine, the unseen, the area in which it makes no sense to speak of evidence. The scene is the wilderness and Moses is keeping his sheep. I have no doubt that some people know the place and others have perhaps walked there and looked curiously at the bushes. There is a bush in Texas and no doubt in many places that at a certain season is red with the leaves of autumn. The Japanese quince is sometimes called the flaming bush, perhaps with the story of Moses in mind. I can assure you that I have no intention of presenting evidence for anything. I am interested in distinguishing this sort of thing, that there might have been evidence that Moses believed that "the angel of the Lord appeared to him in a flame of fire out of the midst of the bush." Jethro, his father-in-law, might have told everyone in the neighborhood that Moses believed this and, what is more, that God called to him out of that bush, and talked to him, explained things to him and finally gave him a commission. He was to go to Egypt and make demands upon a king. Imagine it, a man believing that God Almighty, maker of heaven and earth, talked to him, shepherd in the desert, and chose him, against his inclinations—"I am not eloquent; . . . : for I am slow of speech, and of a slow tongue"— to be the leader of his, God's, own people. Of course, he believed something fantastic. The Maker of the whole world and all the stars having a rendezvous with a dusty keeper of his father-in-law's sheep. Did he believe it? Let us say so. Men have believed the most fantastic things. And he, then, believed it, but not in an idle fashion. One could scarcely do that in an idle fashion—stand before a burning bush with his shoes in his hand and become in an instant, like Abraham, the confidant of God and become the plenipotentiary of the Most High. Is not this grandeur? And yet is this possible? Well, are not the Mormons fantastic and grand? And Moses not only believed, and trembled in his weakness, but became a mighty man, obedient when he went. I am writing as though I knew something, but I am writing only of what is humanly possible. Belief is possible. And such belief! Is there now no evidence possible that the angel of Jehovah appeared to him in a flame of fire? There is no evidence and no evidence possible. It is not that evidence is lacking. Evidence is inconceivable. Did God, the God of Abraham, speak to Moses? Moses believed. But only God knows. If anyone were impertinent enough to seek evidence here, surely he would get the dummy door in his face. Moses believed.

Once again if anyone should ask why I consider this episode in the story of Moses in this way, it is not for the purpose of distinguishing these elements, the human and the divine, in this story, save as I regard this story as exemplifying the form or a certain aspect of the form of the life of the servant of God, for both Jew and Gentile. The Christian in 1968 is also a servant of God, in whom he believes—whether or not like Moses in the shadow of a mountain he comes upon a burning bush. "No man hath seen God." No man hath seen any evidence either. There may be no burning bush in Elmhurst. But there must be one seared conscience. And repentance has been described as "a refining fire." ("The meaning of the world of the believer is not in the world" [Wittgenstein].)

I want now to use one more example. In respect to what I am in the main interested in, this may be superfluous, but I should not like to leave the impression that what I am saying holds only for episodes in the Old Testament. Again the emphasis will be on the distinction between the human and the divine. The following is a familiar passage:

Acts 9. "But Saul, yet breathing threats and slaughter against the disciples of the Lord went unto the high priest and asked of him letters to Damascus. . . . And as he journeyed, it came to pass that he drew nigh unto Damascus: and suddenly there shone round him a light out of heaven: and he fell upon the earth and heard a voice saying unto him, 'Saul, Saul, why persecutest thou me?' And he said, 'Who art thou, Lord?' and he said, 'I am Jesus, whom thou persecutest: But rise and enter into the city and it shall be told thee what thou must do.' And the men that journeyed with him stood speechless hearing the voice, but beholding no man. And Saul arose . . . ."

All of this account is within the range of evidence, of the seen and heard. Again I do not mean that we have any such evidence. We do not. A man, Saul, asks for papers. The secretary of the synagogue might have kept records. There might still have been in the files the request that Saul made and a copy of the letters he requested. On the way "there shone round about him a light out of heaven." We have all read of flying saucers. Those too can be frightening. People say they have seen them and some have even taken pictures. "And he fell to the ground." That too seems natural enough. Now he heard a voice, "Saul, Saul, why persecutest thou me?" People hear voices too. So that is human. In our time there are explanations of such things. It would not have been the first time that men have suffered from sunstroke or delirium of some sort. But Saul does not react in that way. He does not ask, "What is the matter with me?" or "What did I eat for breakfast?" He is overwhelmed, God-struck, and he says: "Who art thou, Lord?" Is it not astounding that he says, not, "What art thou?" but "Who art thou, Lord?" It is at that very instant that he becomes a servant. And he remains a servant throughout his life. We must not, however, forget that it is still Saul who falls "upon the earth," who hears the voice, who responds, and who receives the command: "But rise and enter into the city." Saul did not say, "This is all so sudden and so strange, give us a while to recollect our wits so that we can make an investigation." Later Saul was told "Thou art mad," but it did not now occur to him. Why mad? Obviously, to believe such things. Up to this very minute he knew that Jesus Christ had been crucified, was dead and buried, and finished. Now on his way to persecute those who believed that he was not dead but alive and continuing his work, on the spur of one miraculous moment he himself partakes of this shameful and fantastic superstition. If now we ask: And when Saul asked, "Who art thou, Lord?" was there a Lord and was there one who from now on ordered his life? Or was it all in Saul's head? If the answer [to the first question] is yes, this must be regarded as a confession of faith and as a token too of one's own servitude. Only another servant has a right to say yes. For Saul did not merely nod his head. His falling to the ground may be taken as a sign of his subjection to his Lord. Knowledge is not involved. Lordship is not a matter here of royal purple and a golden seal. "Thy will be done."

Once more the point of this discussion is that there is no room here for evidence. "Who art thou, Lord?" is said by one who in saying it does not make a discovery, as though he noticed something and inferred that Jesus was after all someone important, perhaps Moses or Elijah, as men had said earlier. In this utterance Saul becomes a servant, certainly not knowing what the end would be and, as he would have said, "through the grace of God." It is a mistake to regard Saul as believing at one moment and obeying the next—as though he then said, "Well, I had better."

I should like at this point to make a remark and then another one. Both have some bearing on the matter of evidence. First I must point out an interesting parallel. In the story of Moses we are told that "the angel of Jehovah appeared unto him in a flame of fire out of the midst of a bush. And the bush burned with fire and the bush was not consumed." In the story-account of Saint Paul we are told: "And suddenly there shone round about him a light out of heaven." In the story of Abraham there is nothing to match these incidents. It is striking that the calling of Moses, like that of Saint Paul, has as a part of its setting in the one case "a flame of fire" and in the other "a light out of heaven." In connection with these the temptation may arise to say that they are evidence of God's presence. But to whom are they to serve as evidence? Let us allow, to begin with, that certainly the burning bush served as an occasion for God's intervening in the life of Moses. Moses said, "I will turn aside now, and see this great sight, why the bush is not burned." He turns aside and then Jehovah said, "Moses, Moses." If, accordingly, God uses a burning bush to attract a man's attention, it does not involve that to that man or any man that a bush burns is evidence for this, that God did speak to Moses. The burning bush is simply a part of the story. If, by the way, we regard the burning bush as a miracle, it does not involve that we have discovered that it is a miracle. To regard it as a miracle is neither to have found an explanation nor to have failed in finding an explanation. It is to be filled with wonder at such an event—and not to ask questions about it. In this sense the ordinary, a drop of water or a grain of sand, may strike us not as extraordinary but as miracles. How wonderful! The miracle, however, is not the evidence of anything.

We may say that a Christian and any man called of God have an environment which other men do not have. When a Christian, with the psalmist, looks out upon the heavens and hears them declare the glory of God in flaming red or sees the firmament declare, in the green finery of spring, God's handiwork—he sees the same setting sun and the same expanse of earth and yet he sees something different. When the Christian, again with the psalmist, sings:

Psalm 65 "And the hills are girded with joy
        The pastures are clothed with flocks:

> The valleys also are covered with grain;
> They shout for joy, they also sing."

or

> Psalm 98 "Let the floods clap their hands;
> Let the hills sing for joy together."

or

> "O Jehovah, how manifold are thy works!
> In wisdom hast thou made them all:
> The earth is full of thy riches."

it is not that he has sought out the hills and pastures and valleys and floods and the riches of the earth as evidence for something. It would be better to say that he has drunk of a sacred potion, "the waters of life," and that his life has been made new and with that his new eyes have seen new hills, pastures, valleys, and floods. "The hills girded with Joy" are not evidence that they are God's creation. They are the hills seen by the psalmist or as seen by the psalmist. A transfiguration of the landscape.

Should we ask whether when King David sang, "The Lord is my shepherd," he sang it only after having counted the score, reviewed the evidence? In that case ought we not say that he reviewed the evidence too early and the psalm was premature?

My second remark is a remark about the three passages which I have reviewed. It has struck me that in each of these episodes, God calls and orders a man to do something. There is a command. To Abraham God said, "Go" and Abraham went. To Moses God said, "Now, therefore, go" and Moses went. To Saul, Jesus said, "Rise and enter into the city" and Saul arose. Shall we say that in each of these God reveals himself? I take it that the word "revelation" may give us trouble. How? We may think of revelation, of being revealed, by analogy with revelation or being revealed where what is revealed is seen. You cannot see it; now you can see it. The curtain has been raised. But what are we to make of the revelation of what is unseen and cannot be seen? I have already made some point of saying that evidence is connected with what we can see. What you see is evidence for what you cannot see but what you may see later. But as I have reminded you already, "no man hath seen God" and yet God reveals himself. Now, then, if we say that God revealed himself to Abraham, we can see that God revealed himself to Abraham in the command. But the revelation now does not consist in saying that so-

and-so is the command. *It consists in commanding.* Perhaps I should include promising, seeing that Jehovah also promised Abraham that he would make of him a great nation. For the moment I propose to keep the discussion simple. Later we can add to it. Accordingly the idea of revelation does not involve one's coming to see what one did not see. But it does involve a transformation. One, having been a wild creature, "following the inclination of one's own heart," is now, as I said earlier, made subject to a lord. One's subjection, either in obedience or in disobedience with guilt, makes of the wild creature a new and tame one. Revelation does not involve that God tells someone secrets. God's revelation is a matter of putting one into harness. Once one was one's own but now one belongs, yes, belongs, to a taskmaster. "We are not our own." God's revealing something is God's making something of a mere human being, making him the father of the faithful, making him the leader, lawgiver, judge, and prophet, making him the great apostle to the Gentiles. God's revelation is power. God's revelation is like a man, a very great man, indeed, and greater than that, coming into a man's living room and taking over the direction of that man and that man's life. Perhaps I should include that the man into whose living room the greater comes is humbled before the greater and is willingly subject to the greater as to the higher. So once again we come to what we noticed earlier: the Bible is the story of what God has done and the story of a Christian is the story of what has happened to him. There is the story of Abraham, the story of Moses, the story of Saint Paul.

What occasion is there in this case to ask for evidence? Is it clear that there is only a command and a promise?

If we say that God is *something out of this world*, we must still be careful to keep that conversation in mind.

Should anyone object: It is clear enough what, in each case, Abraham, Moses, and Saint Paul, become, but what of the man next door who is no celebrity and never will make any great stir in the world? Well, the answer is that the fruits of faith are not at all startling in this world. The little man too is a servant, even if he does not walk so tall, does not carry a sword, and does not address the Athenians on Mars Hill. The fruits of faith are not led into the city with twenty-seven or thirty-nine trombones. They come in on pussy-feet. They are quiet. They are the tender virtues: "Put on therefore, as God's elect, holy and beloved, a heart of compassion, kindness, lowliness, meekness, long-suffering; forbearing one another and forgiving each other, if any man have a complaint against any; even as the Lord forgave you, so also do ye; and above all these things put on love which is the bond of perfectness. And let the peace of Christ rule in your hearts to which also you were called in one body: and be ye thankful" (Colossians).

Before I go on I want to present the man who seeks for evidence in the situation in which, as I have presented the subject, he rightly belongs. I include the man who has also discovered such evidence.

Accordingly, imagine such a man meeting Father Abraham, the father of the faithful, on his way from Haran "to go into the land of Canaan." He knows what he is about and so he begins asking Abraham questions: "Why are you going to the land of Canaan?" Father Abraham tells him, "Jehovah said, Get thee out . . . ." Our friend, for he is a friend, is a bit flustered at this, goes on: "Is that so? And what makes you so certain? You may have been taken in. You must know that you ought to have a reason. What are you going to tell the relatives and the philosophers in Haran and Canaan? What justification do you have for trusting—who did you say it was?—in matters as momentous as this? Ur of the Chaldees was good to your father and Haran has been good to you. And here you are on your way to a place you have never even visited. I advise you to seek guarantees. You are going to have a lot of explaining to do. Gods and men, gods as well as men, ought to act as responsibly as banks. In the case of banks you can ask to see the yearly report. Here past performance warrants your depending upon next year's performance. And don't get the idea that justification is by faith. That was Luther's mistake. It is precisely faith that requires justification. Give us now one good reason for your trusting that it was indeed Jehovah who said to you, 'Get thee out of this country . . . .' A voice, yes. But an honest one?" Our friend is indeed here now confronting the father of the faithful. Ordinarily when he speaks freely of evidence and having a reason and justification he is only talking to other talkers, and not to others of whom we might say, "They went," as it is said of Abraham that he went. In any case imagine this further. Father Abraham is disconcerted. He thought for a moment and then he gave our friend a new and inspired tight version of the ontological proof. Our friend was dumbfounded. Where had Father Abraham gone to school? Our friend listened and then he said: "I beg your pardon. Go on to the land of Canaan." Milton, a man, justified the ways of God to man. And that is also what Father Abraham did. God in gratitude made of him a great nation. And that is what is called reverse English. Or should we say "preverse"?

Here is another adventure of our friend: this time he is a defender of the faith. The occasion is that when he appeared with Saint Paul before

Festus and King Agrippa. He appeared in the court as a friend of the court and was asked to speak first. He began speaking of having a reason and justification and defense, learnedly. He quoted from the ancients and then he quoted from some that had not yet been born, the latter more powerful even than necessary. He was eloquent about the life of reason, since one could show with a reason that there was something better than a reason, namely, faith, provided there was always a reason to support saying so. When King Agrippa asked him for reasons why Saint Paul should go about as he was, stirring up trouble, he protested that even though he had not found a reason yet, there must be one. A must-be reason, he said, is just as good as a reason in the hand, the must-be reason being in effect a reason in the bush. Both Festus and King Agrippa applauded this and were ready to set Saint Paul free. Some attendant, however, reminded them that before setting him free, he should be invited to speak. So he was and he gave his defense—reason or justification—and it was shockingly different from anything that our friend had said. He told a story. It must have embarrassed our friend. "Is that a defense?" he whispered to Saint Paul. And Saint Paul said that it was the only defense he had. Curiously, whereas the people in the court had applauded our friend, a rational creature from somewhere in the neighborhood of Mars Hill, Festus could not contain himself and shouted, "Paul, thou art mad," which seems reasonable, considering the story he told. He added, however, "Thy much learning hath made thee mad." That does not seem right. If anything, Saint Paul defended himself like a simpleton. Imagine it, a story for a defense. And what a story!

I have used three excerpts from the stories of Abraham, Moses, and Saint Paul. Someone may say, "And what do we have to do with these stories?" Well, these are heroes of the faith. These are exemplars of the faith. If, accordingly, any man think that he has faith, he must discover in himself what he may also discover in them. So this man is like Abraham, like Moses, like Saint Paul. It is obvious, however, that the man in 1968 has not gone out from Haran, nor demanded of Pharaoh, "Let my people go," nor preached in the synogogue or on Mars Hill. These exploits are, however, incidental to occasions. The essential is that each of them was intimate with the Almighty. Think of it! "And I will come in and sup with him." It is, I know, absurd, that a creature like man should live on intimate terms with the maker of the stars. "And then he made the stars." For notice: Against whom does a man sin, grumble when he grumbles, strike in anger when he strikes? ("Inasmuch as ye do it to one of these, my brethren, ye do it unto me.") To whom does a man confess and pray? Who forgives him? With whom is he reconciled? Who has declared his love for this creature, man? This intimacy takes place in the spirit, in an atmosphere of love. So why do we need these stories? To remind us of what it is to which we are called.

For the present purpose there is something more. These stories may serve to instruct us concerning how we are to speak of faith and of "a reason," and "a defense," *as these expressions are used in the Scriptures.* And the same is true of the word "justifications" and the word "evidence." I have emphasized "as used in the Scriptures" since it is neglect of this or confusion regarding this that has in fact led to the confusions which have occasioned this paper.

In what I have written I have tried to present to you, in terms first of the predicament of people who either ask or answer the question, Is there a God or not? and then in terms of what I have regarded as relevant passages from the Scriptures, the fact that there is no room for the question, And what is the evidence? Admitting, however, that the urge to persist in this question, almost as though one scanned the landscape to search for the evidence, is extremely powerful, the problem arises as to how it is that we do this. It is not, remember, that we look for what is not there. We look for what cannot be there. Neither is it like looking for air in a vacuum. There might be air in the enclosure which is supposed to be a vacuum. It is rather like looking for air in joy, in kindness, in anger. It is said that oil and water do not mix. And so it is with evidence and faith. It must, accordingly, be clear that there is some misunderstanding, and not a superficial misunderstanding, since the urge to inquire for evidence is so strong. This is now what I should like to explain.

It must be obvious to begin with that my exposition can be of no interest to anyone who does not share the interest in those passages from the Scriptures expressed by the phrase "God's word." That is, those stories which I have used, must, in some way, be regarded as exemplary, not only in respect to the characters involved, but also in respect to the language which is employed. And it is important that the language which is employed excludes language which is not employed.

It occurs to me now that it may be well to distinguish among those who seek for evidence. There are those who approach the Scriptures in a hostile manner, with chips on their shoulders, asking not so much for evidence but for what they regard as the fatal admission that none can be given, or at least, that those who believe are helpless in finding any. They can indeed crow. In the shadow-boxing contest they always win. Then there are the others, those who are by no means hostile, but who in seeking for evidence, are misled by the Scriptures themselves, to which Scriptures they are devoted, and are under the illusion that in seeking for evidence they "do God service," helping along the cause of the Scripture by a straw or two straws here or there, helping in this way to move a mountain. These are the people who might listen to a lecture like this, disappointed, of course.

With the former group of thinkers we need not concern ourselves much. They are right when they exclaim "Aha! there is no evidence!" But they nevertheless show in this philosophical hooting that they do not understand. For it does not show understanding when a man asks for evidence when it makes no sense to ask for evidence. All the same the urge is there. And how are we to explain that? Out of what does this misunderstanding arise? Out of the disposition to regard all uses of language as the same. Of course, the range of language within which we may and do ask for evidence and proof is extremely large, and it may seem that what in our lives we share and have in common is like this. We know so much and every year we know more. Knowledge is more and more important. It is an industry. We make knowledge by the light-year. We make so much that we do not have heads enough to store it. We store it in boxes and books and slot machines. This is our preoccupation. Knowledge will save us. And so it will, from ignorance more than any-thing else. It is the pursuit of knowledge that fashions our minds and at the same time cripples us. For it renders us incapable of understanding those uses of language to which we have then become strangers. We can no longer hear "the still small voice," or if we do we ask, "And what is the evidence?" In this way the divine command with promises is lost or frittered away with senseless questions. A man may in this way become an expert on the sounds of insects, the chirp of crickets, the hum of the mosquito, the buzz of the bee—he may have a menagerie of evidence—and yet he may have no ear at all for the still, small voice until it sounds like the blast of the whirlwind. The writer of those notes from the underground complains, "I couldn't even become an insect." And what can knowledge do or what can we do with, knowledge? We might make a mosquito chirp. Anything else? Yes, knowledge is good wholesome entertainment. What do you expect us to do with our leisure? Surfing? Surfing is too exhausting.

What misleads the former class of thinkers—namely, the disposition to regard all language as serving "to convey thoughts"—is no doubt an influence also in the thinking of the latter class of thinkers. It may even be the dominant and pervasive influence. But there are other entanglements connected with the language of the Scriptures itself. I have in mind, especially, confusions surrounding the uses of the word "belief" and those surrounding the uses of the words "reason," "defense," and, as I have heard, the word "justification."

I have now suggested that the word "belief" gives us trouble, and now I will add, no wonder. For the words "belief" and "believe" are used not only in the religious context but in other contexts. And in some of those at least we may say that there is evidence for what one believes. There are, as we know, hunches, forebodings, fears that, intimations, inklings, conjectures, surmises, and so on. Sometimes we hear a man say, "Well, I believe that it will turn out all right, but then, I am an optimist." This "but then I am an optimist" is not likely to persuade anyone. No evidence is presented. Generally if the belief in question is a belief of any moment, concerning something important, we will want to know what reasons there are for his believing that. And what serves him as reasons will commonly be evidence for what he believes. Evidence may be meager or even conclusive. In the latter case all we need is to get Tom, Tom, the piper's son to admit it. "Did you steal the pig?" In many cases we believe upon the basis of some evidence, explore further, and hopefully get to the point where we know. It must now be obvious that the word "believe" in the religious context will certainly tempt the unwary and may tempt too those who should know better.

In the religious context the words "belief" and "obedience" are closely related. The passages from Scriptures I quoted earlier show this. Belief and obedience are not distinct. Perhaps the word "faith" avoids this, but, as we shall see, the warnings of the apostle James in this regard do not bear this out. The use of the word "belief" may have served to corrupt our understanding of the word "faith" as well. There is some apprehension that this misunderstanding has corrupted the preaching of the gospel also. First, there is something you are to believe. Now the temptation ensues, How can one believe without evidence? So one looks for evidence. One cannot believe anything of this sort without a little help from the landscape, without the crutches of a few words on the side. Evidence is the crutch of belief. But faith with a crutch is not faith. Here I have substituted the word "faith" for the word "belief." Does it help? In any case, the apostle James warns us that faith without works, that is, without obedience, is dead. The predicament might be avoided if we noticed and kept in mind the expression "believe in" as a correction of our confusion in connection with the word "believe." It is significant that in the Apostle's Creed we use the expression "I believe in . . . ." and not: "I believe that . . . ." When Saint Paul gave his defense he did not explain how he came to believe that so-and-so as he might have come to prove the Pythagorean Theorem. Had it been a case of believing so-and-so, he might well have kept quiet and no one would have bothered him. What then did Saint Paul do? He explained how he came to be going about preaching—placing his whole life at the disposal of a newly imposed servitude. And how is it otherwise concerned? Well, first a man believes that so-and-so, which is a lot like nodding one's head, "Yes, that is true. Now, let me go back to sleep." Suppose, however, that one believes and is now alarmed. God now presents "an imminent and present danger." Accordingly, one seeks to live his life in conformity with what one believes. God, however, does not in this way come to be involved. The belief, or what is called the belief, intervenes and is like a shield protecting oneself against the direct encounter. One may have heard that God commands so-and-so. Both God and the command are, as it were, held at a distance where they can do no harm. One does not hear God commanding this here and now, "roaring in the index." The belief lets a man sleep. He does not, like Jacob, have to wrestle with an angel throughout the dark night.

What I have now discussed, namely confusion surrounding the uses of the word "belief," is connected with another misunderstanding, namely, that Christianity is a set of doctrines, of propositions, a theory, an explanation. And what can one do with those? Prove them. And who will show you how to do that? Well, Aristotle was a prover and Euclid has been teaching us for 2,000 years. And Saint Paul? Saint Paul tells stories. But what then is Christianity? Christianity is a faith, we all know that. It is also a hope and a fear. It is a promise and a threat. It is a light shining in the darkness. It is a knock at the door. It is a guest at supper. It is coals of fire. It is weeping at a betrayal. It is reconciliation. It is hearing the voice of the shepherd. It is new wine to drink. It is madness. It is a house built on a rock. It is the Truth walking. It is the eternal in rags. It is the finishing touch. It is the lily of the valley. It is the Roysterer son, home again, home again. It is the black sheep found. It is the rich young ruler, sorrowful. It is the widow's mite. It is love rebuffed. It is rosemary for remembrance. It is a lamb slain. It is "a brand plucked out of the fire."

Should I now add that it is a head stuffed with learning?

I am passing on now to consider the second source of the misunderstanding. I mean the second source I mentioned earlier. For this purpose I am going to quote.

Here is the first quotation:

1 Peter 3:15 "Be always ready with your defense whenever you are called to account for the hope that is in you, but make the defense with modesty and respect."

And here is another translation:

"but sanctify in your hearts Christ as Lord; being ready always to give answer to every man that asketh you a reason concerning the hope that is in you."

Here is a second quotation:

Col. 4:6 "Let your speech be always with grace, seasoned with salt, that ye may know how you ought to answer each one."

Another translation is this:

"Let your conversation be always gracious and never insipid; study how best to talk with each person you meet."

The first quotation with the expressions "your defense" and "called to account," and in the other version with the expression "That asketh you a reason," interests me because I know at least one person who, heeding this injunction, busies himself with proofs for the existence of God. So far as I can make out he regards this as a Christian venture. As I suggested earlier "he thinketh that he doeth God service." No doubt there are ever so many others who work hard at this, too, picking the locks on the dummy doors. Curiously, neither Saint Peter nor Saint Paul has furnished these zealous defenders "of the hope that is in them" with any such proofs, and it must be admitted, accordingly, that they did not in their own defense supply what these later defenders now find needful. It is indeed too bad. The world has existed for so many centuries and all this time man has had to get along without a proof for the existence of God—except, of course, for the bogus ones which do nicely for some people. In the face of all this isn't it amazing that Abraham when he was told "Go" went and when Moses was told "Go" he also went. And so too with Saint Peter and with Saint Paul? Perhaps the explanation is that each of them in his time did prove the existence of God so that when God did put each one of them under orders it was no surprise. And by that time the proof had served its purpose and so each of them promptly forgot it. They seem to have done better in the old days. They must have been very clever, so clever that even Kant must have said, "Now, here is a proof I can't touch. It is superb or superperb." If ever the Bible is revised and, one might say, improved, there should be a new first book, a sort of Pre-Genesis written by an ante-Moses. It seems no more than reasonable that when, as we now do, we come to the verse, "In the beginning God . . . ," just like that, out of the blue, there should have been some preparation. We should know what to expect. We should not have to worry ourselves with Fyodor about such a question: "Is there a God or not?" or "Is there a beginning or not?" If we had a new first book, Pre-Genesis, to take care of such questions, proving the existence of God out of a pop-gun, neat and with a click, and so no one would ever have to ask that question or if he did he could be referred to Pre-Genesis, Chapter I, how happy we should be! This would make reading the Bible so much more comfortable. Imagine how it would be if you went to the theater and the main character in the play—at least, he was said to be the main character, and his name was written large in the lists of the cast—that character never appeared on the stage at all. Naturally some people would be suspicious that there was no such character. In that case it might be arranged to have that character appear in a Prologue, in person, and perhaps, making a short speech, explain why he never appeared on the stage. That should satisfy all those suspicious people who asked, Is there a main character in the play or not? And it is some such service that I propose for my new first book of the Bible. There does seem to be a need for that book. If we had that book we should not be distressed by such conversations as precipitated this discussion. And our philosophers could join the peace corps.

I have now said enough to indicate how men, especially the bright ones, misunderstood such expressions as "your defense," "a reason," and another word they are fond of, namely, the word "justification." They know well enough how Euclid might have been "ready with a defense" when called to account, not for a hope, but for something he said, and so they yearn to account for the hope in the same way. Euclid did it with a proof and that was final. They know well enough how scientists answer each other by presenting evidence and they yearn for the respect and respectability of scientists, giving such an answer to every man that asketh . . . a reason such as scientists have made respectable, namely evidence. What do they forget? They forget that a hope is not a proposition. The apostle is enjoining those to whom he writes to "be always ready with your defense whenever you are called to account for the hope that is in you. . . ." And what then is such a defense like? As one might expect, one must consult the same Scriptures to find out. It is Saint Paul whose defense is the exemplary defense. Saint Paul tells the story; I realize that this defense is to us who are used to other defenses an extraordinary performance. And only a God-stricken man would give such a defense, a madman, indeed as Festus said. As I have intimated before, Saint Paul had never had the benefit of the elegance, "trippingly on the tongue" or page proofs of Euclid nor that of the microscopic test tube with which we are all familiar. If he had, he would no doubt have told a different story or no story at all. All the same if we are to learn from the Scriptures what the defense of a hope is like or what a reason is, then we too must learn from Saint Paul. Saint Paul was a witness. A witness is one who has seen and heard. And what one has seen and heard is a happening. It is true, of course, that not everyone who was there saw and heard what the witness saw and heard. For to the witness it was revealed. So, of course, there was nothing to tell but the story, "but when the fulness of time came, God sent forth his son. . . . that he might redeem . . ." (Galatians, Ch. 4).

I want before I finish to remind you of a familiar word about faith, namely, "Now faith is the substance of things hoped for, the evidence of things not seen." I realize that more recent translations are different from this. Here is another: "Now faith is the assurance of things hoped for, the conviction of things not seen." And here is another: "And what is faith? Faith gives substance to our hopes, and makes us certain of realities we do not see." My intention, however, was not to quote Scripture. I wanted quite on my own to say that faith is the evidence. And yet I did not so much want to say this as to use that sentence, and to use it in such a way as to show that even faith is not evidence. Consider then that there is someone to whom the unseen has been preached. And now, as is natural enough, he wants evidence and seeks for this. And where now should he look? Even a bird or a flower may tempt him. The Maker of the bird, especially the gaudiest bird, that startles us with a flash in the greenery, is certainly unseen. Indeed, and yet the peacock and the bird of paradise are dumb. Should we say that their feathers are loud and so loud we cannot understand or are so soft they only hum or murmur? What does the peacock or the fuzzy little chick have to say about the God of Abraham, Isaac, and Jacob? Shall we direct this man, then, to consider the stars? What have the stars to say? Or a shooting star? Or the northern lights? I have not forgotten Saint Augustine. He asked the earth and it answered, "I am not He." "I asked the sea and the deeps and the creeping things . . . . I asked the breezy air and the universal air with its inhabitants. . . . I asked the heavens, the sun, moon, and stars." They all answered, "We are not He." "I answered: 'Tell me something about Him.'" "And with a loud voice they exclaimed: 'He made us.'" Notice that in this conversation between Saint Augustine and the earth and the sea and the air and the heavens (earth, water, air, and fire), nothing is said about evidence. Saint Augustine does not say, "From these facts we can draw a conclusion." Nor does he say that the stars presented evidence as though they meant to take part in a meeting of astronomers, disputing with astronomer Halley and astronomer Galileo—"their beauty was their reply." Nature is treated like a witness. "He made us." This beauty of the earth screams, exclaims. It does not argue. Nature startles, stamps its foot, claps its hands, shouts for joy, makes a glad noise, roars in majestic thunder, is terrible in the lightning and the storm.

I want to return to the sentence with which I began: "Faith is the evidence." The beauty of the earth speaks. "But they only understand it who compare the voice received without with the truth within." Only those ready to receive receive. Only those who wonder wonder. I remarked earlier that Saint Augustine converses with creeping things and birds and stars *as witnesses*. By no means are these philosophers. There are, however, other witnesses. "Wherefore, seeing we also are compassed about with so great a cloud of witnesses. . . ." These witnesses are the men of faith. And we are now prepared to notice the difference. The man of faith is not a creeping thing, nor that great leviathan, nor a star. All these are dumb witnesses. "Their beauty is their voice." But the man of faith can speak. He is articulate. As a witness he is like a talking star. It was, by the way, a star that led the wise men to the inn at Bethlehem, where the Word lay in the manger. But I must return to the point. As the flower of the field is a witness, a reminder, and not evidence, so too the man of faith is a witness and not evidence. The man of faith is an arresting creature along with the other wonders in the world, a talking wonder. In him we may see the hope and the assurance and the conviction, but he speaks to us of the things that are Unseen. This must now be obvious. It won't do to say: "He believes so-and-so and so so-and-so must be true," as though his believing were evidence of what he believed. He is a witness, but a witness not just in speaking. His life is the witness, the fruits of the spirit.

The Invisible

This paper was delivered at the Howard W. Hintz Memorial Lecture at the University of Arizona in 1969. Bouwsma was invited to present a lecture "giving some impression of how a philosopher in the Wittgenstein tradition might go about 'doing philosophy' in this area [philosophy of religion]." The first part of the manuscript reads as a unified whole, though as a lecture, and we have presented it as such. The remainder consists of segments added at several later dates (although the whole paper was probably read at Arizona). We edited those segments and include here the last dated section only, which returns to the themes of "the invisible" and faith as "the substance of things unseen." The omitted sections portray the belief of Noah, Abraham, and Moses as a reminder of how the "Invisible Stranger" is identified and are similar in content to the discussion in the previous paper.

A lecture is something that is read. In this scnsc what I am about to read is a lecture. I am a reader and I read a reading. Ordinarily, however, a lecture is one thought, a thought as long as the lecture, which may be quite a long thought. From this, one can see at once that there are five-minute thoughts, ten-minute thoughts, and even thoughts an hour long. An hour-long thought is a reasonably long thought. There are, accordingly, thinkers who think short thoughts and thinkers who think long thoughts. I am a short-thought thinker who envies long-thought thinkers. Why am I telling you all this? In order that you may be prepared to hear a reading of short thoughts I had hoped all along that, of short thoughts which I was sure I could think, I could compose one long thought which I would then manage to think. But whenever I tried to put the short thoughts together and I tried to think them as one long thought, the together short thoughts fell apart and I was reduced again to thinking short thoughts. This distressed me. I was, however, lifted up and fortified with another short thought; namely, that there must be others who think only short thoughts and they would not only sympathize with me but would agreeably and comfortably think short thoughts with me. Socrates, you may remember, complained of this same disability. He said that he could think only short thoughts and pleaded with Protagoras, who was a long-thought thinker but who said he could think thoughts of any length, both long and short, to please cut them short. I should not like anyone to think that I have in mind long-winded and short-winded thinkers, but now that I think of it, I do not much care. I am all out of breath.

With this in mind I can also say that this lecture has a beginning but no end, and also no middle—at least not in my lifetime.

There is no subject more bewildering and more frustrating than the subject of religion or, as in the present circumstances, than Christianity. And this is because of the role of the Scriptures. I might say that this is because we do not know how to read the Scriptures, or at any rate, some of us do not. That would not be so bad, if only there were some among us who not only could read but who could discuss the language of the Scriptures, could explain it to us, in such a way that we could learn to read it too. But where are the teachers to whom we are to go? There are many teachers and so we are once more bewildered, not only by the Scriptures, but by the too many teachers. It is with the teachers as with the cooks. The cooks spoil the broth. I do not know whether this has always been the case. I have an idea that it has been so. In the early days of the church the writers of the epistles had repeatedly to correct misunderstandings, particularly concerning faith and the keeping of the law. Their problems, however, may not have been either so serious or so basic as ours. And we are concerned with ours. I have already suggested that we do not know how to read. By this I do not mean that we open the book, try to read, discover that we cannot, and then close the book. This we might do, were we to open a book in a foreign language. "I cannot read this. It's all Greek to me," or all Hebrew, as the case might be. But the case is not like that. The words are familiar. They are English. And when we come upon an unfamiliar word we can find out what it means. In this way we are provided with all the help we need. Our troubles are of another kind. We open the book. We read. The words are familiar. We are well acquainted with the whole book, perhaps too well acquainted. Kierkegaard writes of obtaining "a little peace for the weary Christian terminology, a rest of which it may stand greatly in need, unfathomable and calmly profound as it is in itself, but made breathless and almost unmeaning in current usage. . . . Christianity tossed about and perplexed in current speech." So we read and we understand—so we think. If then we do not understand, we must consider how this can be, that we should read a book with which we could scarcely be more familiar—at any rate, it is not either unfamiliarity or ignorance that would account for the illusion of understanding. And yet we do not understand. It may be, of course, that the illusion of understanding what we read and write or say is not uncommon. Some people may even make a career of it, make of it a specialty.

Here, at any rate, is a matter of deep concern to some people, that by way of the illusion of understanding men should be deprived of understanding what it is of such importance that they should understand. It is as though a man opened a door to a room where there is nothing, under the illusion that he had opened a door and entered a room in which there was great treasure. The Scriptures are the door. Let us take notice of language concerning which there is no such problem. There is our language, the language we do understand. We use it. We write the books. We coin the words as we need them. We are almost virtuosos in this language. We pun. We play on words. We make jokes. It is ours. And what do we do with it? We tell stories. We write novels. We write biographies. We write history. We publish books on what we found in Mexico and South America. We tell the world what we have found out about the stars. You and I know the names of many authors. They are people like us. If we read books or read a magazine or a newspaper and do not understand, ordinarily we are aware of this and can find out what we need to find out; if we do not understand and think we do, it is not a matter of importance. It may be that our misunderstanding will be discovered and we will come to understand. And what now does this depend on? There is the one community of agreement within which we understand and misunderstand one another. It is our language. Within it we move and speak and write and understand and have our being. I do not mean by this only that we agree in our vocabulary. There is something more subtle. We undo what it is we do speaking and writing. When you tell a joke I get the point. When you explain it I get the explanation, though I may lose the point, not of the explanation but of the joke. When you give a demonstration, I see. And so on. We have a common background and common interests of which our language is the medium in which we get on together. I must emphasize that it is we whose language this is. We are at home in it. It is our native land, our city, our intimate surroundings. We live here. We are the masters.

Now consider the Scriptures. The Scriptures are described in a variety of phrases: "The Holy Bible," the "Sacred Scriptures," "God's Word," and so on. "God's word," "the divinely inspired word"—think of that. Numb. We are not like Noah, like Abraham, like Moses. And who wrote the Scriptures? Well, we can say either that God wrote those books or that those inspired men did. Somehow we have got to get the idea of God's word in here. It isn't the first time God wrote. He also wrote the law on those two tablets of stone that Moses brought down from the mountain. This may seem a plainer case of authorship. If, however, God or a man has an amanuensis, whose word is this the amanuensis writes (or, who is the author)? I realize that I have in writing in this way already entered the twilight zone of language. We are also acquainted with the expression "the hand of God," and in Omar Khayyam there is "The moving finger writes." The language now seems almost to melt away. All those expressions having a definite form, all expressions but ours in our common language where we live, such expressions as "wrote" and "author" and "finger" are now almost form-less. And yet this is the language of Scripture. And now I want to notice something more formidable. It isn't now that we are at a loss because we lack the vocabulary, as though we should find a more suitable word than "God wrote." I reminded myself in the pages above that we are masters of our language, being masters in our own house. I did not mean that anyone can tamper with the language as he pleases. It is *we* who are masters in our use of it. I also said that this is rooted in the community of interest and understanding. I can understand what you are saying and I can understand and can respond to what you are doing since we are so much like one another. We are human beings together.

Now consider again the Scriptures. We have already noticed that the vocabulary is nothing unusual. Nearly all the words are ordinary. "In the beginning God created the heavens and the earth"—no big words there, no technical vocabulary. "The Lord is my shepherd: I shall not want"—it's all simple. But for all that there is no book like this one. I want to try to explain this. I said earlier that in connection with the language we all understand, we are human beings together. Our com-mon human nature is the basis of our understanding one another. But now we are no longer in the market place or in the school. In the Scriptures there is always a stronger, an invisible stranger, an unknown. He is there at the end. One might say that the book is his biography. Notice again how I slip into saying what cannot be so—God's biogra-phy—imagine it! This is the language we use about man, and in that context we can also speak of God's obituary, and as soon as we do this we are either in the midst of ambiguity or blasphemy. I am not unaware that God is dead, though there has been some question as to what god this is. This god looks a lot like some people. Mistaken identity. I must return to the "Invisible Stranger." Throughout the Bible this Invisible Stranger, the Unknown, dominates. Were this a novel, one would say that he is the main character. He speaks and he does. How strange! There are these human beings, who are like us, creatures of dust, and this Invisible Stranger—"No man hath seen God"—and this Invisible Stranger keeps in close contact with these human beings. The generations pass and a new generation comes, but the Invisible Stranger continues, as it were, to communicate with them. And what is more he sees to the record. That is, he sees to it that some man takes down the story— as he dictates it. If God is not the author we might as well forget it unless we are interested in holy bric-a-brac. God, the Invisible Stranger, does not forget. I am, I think, writing of the Scriptures from within. This is one way of trying to grasp the role of the Scriptures in the Christian community.

Now we come upon this problem: That we can understand the language in the market place and in our schools was said to depend upon our being human beings together, not only with the same background of language, but with the same interests or interests we all understand. But how now understand the language and, I think, I should add the goings-on in a community in which one member of that community is an Invisible Stranger, who not only is a member of that community, but is dominant in word and deed? If what I said earlier is right, then anyone who is to live in that community with that stranger must understand, not only what is said, as we understand that where we live, but must in another sense understand that stranger. This is to understand God which may be interpreted as understanding God's interests in, God's designs upon, man, the Creature. It may well be that any human being who lived in this community, Moses, for instance, or David, the king, or a prophet, would have no difficulty. He would not be puzzled or respond with the question "But what do you mean?" But if we were to ask, "How is it you can understand God?" the answer might be, "As God provided the sacrifice for Abraham, so too he provided the understanding."

Early in reading this paper I said that we do not know how to read the Scriptures. I think I had better say that we cannot say what understanding the Scriptures is. In the sense in which I was saying that we do not know how to read the Scriptures there is also no human being who can teach us. The idea is that when God speaks or God writes only God himself can give us the understanding. Presumably this is not something in the head. There is the prayer "Give me, O Lord, an understanding heart" that may remind us of Pascal's sentence: "The heart has its reasons which the reason does not know." I would not presume to explain this any further than to notice that the understanding of the Scriptures is not at all like understanding the differential calculus or analytical geometry. Let me repeat: God does not speak or write English or any other earthly language, no matter how much like English or any other language the language of Scripture looks like and sounds like English. I realize that this sounds paradoxical and like the divine language is almost unintelligible. I would like to make this quite clear, though I anticipate that I will fail. In order to reassure myself that I am not talking "with a mouth full of hot mush" I am going to provide myself with a modicum of respectability by quoting a passage from Kierkegaard:

> Suppose Christianity to be a mystery. . . . Suppose a revelation must be a mystery. . . . Suppose that it were after all a blessed thing, critically situated in the extreme press of existence, to sustain a relation to this mystery without understanding it, merely as a believer. Suppose Christianity never intended to be understood. . . . Suppose it refuses to be understood and that the maximum of understanding which could come in question is to understand that it cannot be understood.[1]

I am, accordingly, trying to understand this passage by considering a passage of Scripture. In respect to it I am going to ask, "Do we understand this?"

Before I go on to do that I want to take notice of an ambiguity in the use of the word "understanding." Of Christianity Kierkegaard in this passage says that it cannot be understood. There must be something in the language to show this. But Kierkegaard also speaks of a misunderstanding and that suggests at least a correct understanding. Though this may be misleading, since what would then be a correct understanding would not be at all correlative to the misunderstanding, nothing like "I thought you said 'Go right' when you said 'Go left.'" I'll just suggest that a caress is nothing like a weather report. There are caressing words as every girl knows. There are also cold facts—"It is now 100 degrees in the shade." To treat a caressing word as something to be checked on the thermometer or on the caressometer would show a misunderstanding. What are you doing? Checking.

I want now to consider a passage of Scripture. We can begin with the

---

1. Soren Kierkegaard, *Concluding Unscientific Postscript*, trans. David Swensen (Princeton, N.J.: Princeton University Press, 1941), p. 191 f.

first in the Scriptures: *"In the beginning God created the heavens and the earth."* This sentence in the Scriptures is pretty well insulated against prying questions—but not altogether. The words "God" and "created" are almost foreign words. They might then have prevented any penetration. The sentence is almost like a seal. Now then do we understand? We may say, "No, but we can try." We are acquainted with spontaneous generation. There is life from nothing in the rain barrel, and if you have rags in the corner long enough and at the right tempera- ture a mouse or mice will come out of those rags. Worms out of rain water and a mouse out of rags is as good as something out of nothing. And in this way we approach understanding. It makes understanding easier when it comes, though the idea of God with a rain barrel or God with a pile of rags is a bit disconcerting. Besides, this was in the begin- ning before there was rain and before there were rags. This gives rise to other questions. In the beginning, when was that? Men have figured this out too. From the birth of Christ to Moses, going back, was two thou- sand years, that is two thousand years with the law. And before Moses, how many years to the beginning? Two thousand years. There have been more accurate measurements of the times, before, with, and after the giving of the law on Mount Sinai. There have been other questions designed to embarrass the simple: "And what was God doing before the beginning, before He created the world?" I mean by the simple, those who do not ask these questions, not because they are not bright enough, though being bright is a perpetual temptation, but because they are subdued, overwhelmed—should I say "poor in spirit"? But the most crucial barrier remains. Who created? God created. And who is that? I am inclined to answer, *"Who* is that." In other words, "It is who." And that is very much like, "I am that I am," which is like silence, like a door slammed shut. There are other serious, mocking questions which have arisen in connection with the story of Creation. There is the passage in *The Brothers Karamazov:*

> Grigory taught him to read and write and when he was twelve years old, began teaching him the scriptures. But this teaching came to nothing. At the second or third lesson the boy suddenly grinned.
> "What's that for?" asked Grigory threateningly from under his spectacles.
> "Oh, nothing. God created light on the first day, and the sun, moon, and stars on the fourth day. Where did the light come from on the first day?"
> Grigory was thunderstruck. The boy looked sarcastically at his teacher. There was something positively condescending in his expression. Grigory could

not restrain himself. "I'll show you where," he cried, and gave the boy a violent slap on the cheek.[2]

Here is another nice problem: "And God called the light Day and the darkness he called Night." Ah! Then since there was as yet no sun and no moon and no revolutions of the earth around the sun, how long were those days and those nights? Twelve-hour day. Twenty-four day and night; a thousand-year day? "A thousand years are with him as one day": a geological age—a very, very long time?

In the foregoing I have tried to remind us of the overwhelming character of the Scriptures, a book in which the Invisible Stranger plays that dominant role. I meant also to insist that God in this book, or God speaking through this book, requires of men a special reading, and that this, particularly among the learned, the wise in this world, involves a constant struggle against habits of mind and understanding. We know so much and have developed critical faculties suited to what we read and study. We are not only tempted but do, as a matter of course, read the Scriptures by analogy with what we so obviously understand. And this habitual mode of understanding may be fixed and fortified by our saying aloud that language is designed to communicate what is so. Carried over into the reading of Scriptures this leads to our noticing ever so many things we do not understand. This language on the surface is the language of biography or history or that of a story. "In the beginning" is very much like "Once upon a time," and this is very much like "It was in the spring, the season for flowers in the year 1, just the right time for a creation whim." And so too with the language that follows. We are not however naive now. We are not simple. And we do not want to be taken in. We have learned to be careful. We may even have become suspicious. We have been educated in science, and it doesn't take a genius to see that Genesis is less than a masterpiece of science, even of children's science. That boy of twelve may represent us pretty well: "God created the light on the first day, and the sun and the moon and the stars on the fourth day. Where did the light come from on the first day?" There is a rational boy for you! Disregarding the animus in that boy's asking that question, we might say that he got slapped, not for being featherless as a featherless biped, but as Aristotle also recognized, for being rational as a rational animal.

2. Fyodor Dostoevsky, *The Brothers Karamazov*, trans. Constance Garnett (New York: Norton, 1976), pp. 112–13.

Obviously literature like this cannot compete with Newton and Darwin and Einstein and that great cloud of witnesses who today continue to generate the facts, the facts, with the aid of money and machines. So it isn't science. We can learn nothing from it. What shall we do with it? We can ignore it. That is no doubt what most people do. We put it on the shelf—it may even make a handsome book, it gathers holy dust—and forget it. That seems a good idea. There's no use reading a book like that if you can learn nothing from it, unless one might on occasion be amused by it. But TV offers us enough of that without having to spend ourselves with effort. Effortless amusement is the best. Of course, one might still want to read a little now and then to remind ourselves of how men who could read spent their time before civilization and the higher mind came along. On the whole, however, we have neither time nor inclination for such relics. Of course, we are not to stand in the way of some people, historians and linguists, scholars of various sorts, poring over the language of the book and digging holes in Palestine, to probe the subsoil for the walls of Jericho and, perhaps, finding a few battered trumpets and even some now muted shouts that brought the walls down. Who knows? Men pored over the Iliad too, the grammarians and adventurers, and they did find Troy. Too bad they didn't find Agamemnon. They might have found out some interesting things about that wonder horse.

If anyone should think that in writing this I have a few friends among the scientists, and it is those I am thinking of, he would be wrong, even though I might be tempted on some occasion to say, "See, I was right. The Scriptures are on the shelf." But some among the scientists would not have recognized the allusion to the walls of Jericho and the trumpets and the shouts. Some others might have asked: "And who was Agamemnon?" and "What is Troy?" Trojans in California he might have heard of, but what is Troy? And Utica he might have heard of, but where is Troy? As for the wooden horse, it reminded him of the wooden locomotive set up in the park for the children to play on. In any case, what I wrote was purely apriori. If anyone is going to read the Scriptures in the way in which I described it, as pre-primitive science, leaving God out, then the book must remain unintelligible. "Leave it alone. Forget it."

If what I wrote above is right then there must be still a fourth way of reading the Scriptures. If in trying to describe this I should succeed, such a description is not to be understood as a recommendation or a defense. I am not going to say: "This is the right way," as though this would be intelligible to anyone who read the Scriptures in one of the other ways.

Still I might say that the Scriptures themselves provide directions for such a reading of the Scriptures.

Here then is an account. Scriptures or no Scriptures, man is an amazing creation—to himself, of course. Were he made, one might exclaim that he was "fearfully and wonderfully made." Let us say that he came into the world with the feeling that something is missing. This should not be hard given, of course, something is missing. We might imagine a world in which everybody came into the world and was laid in a basket to which a small booklet was attached—with a blue ribbon, pink for girl babies—a manual of instructions for one's life. It would provide such instructions as no man could have provided either for himself or for another. It would give a sort of preamble, too, describing an environment that no baby, young or old, could discover for himself. As we know, there are at present no such manuals. A long time ago, let us suppose, there were such manuals. For a long time now, however, babies have come into the world restless and they grew up restless, because the manuals were not there. One might say that they remembered the long ago age when the manuals were there, but they could not have said what it was they remembered. Parents might say, "The baby remembers something and that keeps the baby upset." The parents may be upset, too, and cannot supply the missing manual. They do not know what is missing. When the restlessness becomes acute the parents in various ways divert the child. They say, "Ah! What is missing is knowledge." So they take the baby out of the basket and send it to school where there are many books. Other parents say, "Poor child, he needs crayons and color books and piano lessons and a dancing teacher." So they supply what is missing. What the child did not have is not necessarily what is missing. Still other parents say, "Our baby misses rules and a rod, otherwise the baby will not know where to walk. It may fall into the brambles or bruise its foot against a stone." So they make the baby walk in a narrow path. These are, however, only diversions. The nameless ache of the memory of those booklets tied with the pink and the blue ribbons remains. This memory might also be "original memory," named after another original, the original original, "original sin."

Let us now imagine such a grown-up baby whose memory has not been overgrown with the diversions with which it has been surrounded. One day he comes upon the Bible and reads, and he now exclaims, "Ah, the manual, the manual!" If that exclamation should sound like another "Emmanuel," that is more than a happy coincidence, since the word means "God with us." And that suggests that what was once represented as tied to the basket with a blue ribbon might also have been represented as perched over the basket in the form of a dove. Now, however, the real problem begins. For the problem for the baby was not simply one of having his memory stirred so that now he could say what it was he remembered. Having come upon what he remembered, now he could begin to live—since the manual was for that, to instruct him on how to live. And if the manual itself was missing before this, the manual now discovered would also discover to him what else was missing. If a human being is introduced to a new world, then with a new world a new creature and a new life begins. This is what it is so difficult to represent.

In dwelling on these cases I have without intending to do so come close to the perspective of the writer of the letter to the Hebrews. The Hebrews would have understood. Remember Noah, remember Abraham, remember Moses. Why? In order that you may not lose heart. "Cast not away therefore your confidence . . . . For you have need of patience." Then follows that dithyramb of faith beginning, "Now faith is the substance of things hoped for, the evidence of things not seen," celebrating the power of faith. "By faith Noah, being warned of God of things not seen as yet, moved with fear, prepared an ark to the saving of his house;" "By faith Abraham obeyed when he was called to go out to a place which he was to receive an inheritance; and he went and not knowing where he was to go;" and, "By faith Moses . . . ."

In my comments on the passages concerning these heroes of faith I have made a few comments concerning the conception of God, the nature of the hero, and in passing, concerning the nature of belief. The last, belief in God, is the strangest thing. Imagine it—a human being believing in God! I do not know, however, that I should consider this strange since I cannot yet get clear concerning what it is. I do not mean to say that it is not common. It struck me now that in those early chapters nothing is said about belief. We are told—and who could have told us?—"And God said to Noah." We are not told, "And Noah believed that God said to him [Noah]." I suppose were Noah himself to have spoken of this he would have said, "And God said to me. . . ." Had Noah one morning announced to his sons, "I believe God said to me, 'Build thee an ark,'" his sons would very likely have said, "You had better wait until you are sure. Then we will help." But there was no waiting and no epistemological sophistication which required that Noah should have made this distinction. This does introduce a novel question concerning belief in general and religious belief in particular. In that imaginary exchange between Noah and his sons where Noah is represented as saying, "I believe God said to me . . . ," one might be inclined to intercede with, "and how could you not be sure," and the response might be, "Well, I can't figure out now whether God said to me or whether I only dreamed that God said to me. I remember the very words he said, however, and I seldom remember the words said to me in dreams. So I've about made up my mind and I believe God spoke to me." This brings out one more feature of this communication between God and man. Noah has no such access to God as would allow him to ask, "And, Lord, did you say something to me or did I dream it?" If God did say something it would scarcely do for man to say, "I forgot," or "I did not hear." "I heard when you spoke, but I could not make it out." (Who said that God spoke only in riddles?)

My immediate interest here was to notice that the word "believe" did not occur in the language of these stories of the heroes of faith. It is not said, "And Noah believed," or "Abraham believed," or "Moses believed," which would show then that we were especially to attend to that. After all these men are heroes, and heroes are men of deeds, and so we should naturally focus on what these men did. Noah built the ark. Abraham went into a far country. Moses went boldly to King Pharoah and said, "Let my people go." Of course, another man may have built an ark. Many a man has gone into a far country and never come back. Other men have spoken boldly to a king. The difference we may say lies in that what each of these men did he did in obedience. God said, "Build," and Noah built. God said, "Go," and Abraham went. Accordingly it would seem that a more appropriate description of these heroes is "Heroes of Obedience." We must bear in mind that such obedience was a hero's work, obedience against what one might consider one's own better judgment. "Rain? An ark for the flood?" "A far country." The hero, however, is judged a hero by God, and God requires obedience from every hero no matter how smart he is. His being smart may only make his obedience that much more difficult. After all a man does respect his own judgment. This, then, would be the normal understanding. Noah is a hero. Why? He obeyed. That makes him a hero of obedience. But he is called a hero of faith. And there must be something in that description which we have missed.

In what I wrote above I said that I found it especially inviting to use those simple and, one might suppose, primitive examples of the religious life, "and God said unto Noah." It is as simple as that, as simple as Noah walking down the street and meeting Lamech, and Lamech saying unto Noah, "Better take your raincoat." No one would say that there was anything heroic about Noah going back into the house and taking up his raincoat. But God is not Lamech, not the man who lives in the next street and is a relative too. Anyone in 1969 who might give this a little thought would probably find this an expression of simplemindedness on Noah's part, so much like a child, without any troublesome questioning, charming in a child. We may in this connection be reminded of this: "except ye become as little children, ye cannot enter the kingdom of heaven." Following this suggestion, we should not so much describe Noah and Abraham and Moses as Heroes of Obedience, as Heroes of Simplicity, even Heroes of Naivete. But that would be paradoxical. The hero of Naivete! A baby cannot be a hero. There is, however, another possibility. The sentence "And God said to Noah" may be regarded as an understatement, or a statement that leaves much unsaid. For though one cannot enter the kingdom of heaven, except he become as a little one, the condition of remaining there is that he be a hero, that he endure the ordeal of faith. It may be easy to fall in love, how otherwise can one be in love? But to remain faithful to the vow one made in the heyday of the ecstasy may require resolution and strength. Following this suggestion, it was a mistake to regard the hero of faith as one who became a hero in one moment or in five minutes. Faith is rather like a task undertaken and carried out, a venture, a life and an ordeal, a continuing ordeal and triumph.

Have I now let the rhetoric run away with me? I think not. I am suggesting now that faith is to be understood in terms of the life so fashioned, just as the mustard seed is to be understood only in terms of "that least of seeds which when it is grown is the greatest among herbs and becometh a tree."

In the eleventh chapter of Hebrews what has now struck me is the emphasis on the Invisible. "Faith" itself is said to be "The substance of things hoped for, the evidence of things not seen." So the man of faith is that substance, might one also say the power? And that evidence. He is the witness. Of what? Of the Invisible. "Through faith we understand that the worlds were framed by the Word of God so that the things which are seen were not made of things which do appear." The contrast between the seen and the unseen is continued, "a more excellent sacrifice"—what would make it so? The invisible, "for he that cometh to God (The Unseen) must believe that he is." "By faith Noah being warned of things not seen." Abraham was called by God and "looked for a city which hath foundations whose builder and maker is God." Of them all it was said, "They desire a better country, that is, a heavenly one . . . for God hath prepared for them a city." "By faith, he [Moses] forsook Egypt, not fearing the wrath of the king; for he endured, as seeing *him who is invisible.*" The man of faith, the man who lives by faith, is the man who sees with the rest of the seeing among the seeing, seeing the seen. But he lives under orders of, is sustained by, is loved and inspired by, the unseen which the seeing may not see. Faith is memory of the unseen which he has seen and is the enduring access to it throughout his life. There is, of course, a door to the unseen—not words, but the living word.

If now someone should ask, "And in what form is the Invisible active in the world in 1969?" the answer is, "There is a holy spirit haunting men's lives even now through the word, reminding men of him whose life and death and words and resurrection make demands upon men, touching their hearts and consciences, accusing them, goading them, inviting them, coaxing them, lifting them up." To believe in the Invisible One is not only to believe that there is the Invisible but to be subject to the Invisible, to be haunted by, to be demanded of—"If you love me you will keep my commandments,"—to be touched by, accused by a man who had it in his power to make such a gift. Indeed we may describe this belief as belief in the mission impossible. But, of course, with God all things are possible, even that of making of a creature who cannot even withstand a cold or miss on occasion stubbing his toe, an immortal. A man who believes that he is one of those who is marked for such immortality, must indeed be transformed by that prospect. But who could believe it? That impossibility is also possible.

Anselm's Argument

For why do we have our philosophers,
if not to make supernatural things
trivial and commonplace?

Kierkegaard, *Philosophical Fragments*

This paper was written for a series of lectures at Notre Dame University entitled the "Perspectives in Philosophy Lecture Series" in 1966–67. The other participants that year were Stephen Körner, Martin Versfeld, A. J. Ayer, and Stephen Pepper. Bouwsma presented two other papers during his stay there: "Double Talk, Jackie Vernon and X," and "I Think I Am." The lectures for that year are collected in *The Nature of Philosophical Inquiry*, edited by Joseph Bobik (Notre Dame, Ind.: University of Notre Dame Press, 1970). This essay shows Bouwsma's techniques at work on a classical argument in philosophy of religion.

They say that to unscramble an egg is very difficult, that even with all the king's horses and all the king's men one is likely to fail. Imagine, then, how much more difficult it must be to unscramble the scramble of a dozen eggs! In this case, with even the help of all the kings themselves, one can scarcely hope to succeed. And yet that is something like what I propose to do: to restore out of the scramble, a number of eggs, whole and sunny-side up. The scramble I have in mind is the ontological proof, the most bewildering and tantalizing, and neat and compact bit of scramble in the history of philosophy. The only piece that rivals it for complexity and apparent simplicity is the argument of Berkeley. They are both magnificent in both respects, and Anselm's argument looks least like a scramble.

The following summary of the argument may serve to guide the course of the discussion. Nearly all of this will be quoted. The argument is presented by Anselm in the course of a meditation which begins, "And, indeed, we believe that thou art a Being than which none greater can be conceived." This sentence contains the key phrase in the argument. He goes on, "Or is there no such nature, since 'the fool hath said in his heart, There is no God'? But, at any rate, this very fool, when he hears of this Being of which I speak—a being than which none greater can be conceived—understands what he hears, and what he understands is in his understanding; although he does not understand it to exist."

After a paragraph of explanation, he goes on:

Hence even the fool is convinced that something exists in the understanding, at least, than which nothing greater can be conceived. For when he hears of this, he understands it. And whatever is understood is in the understanding. And assuredly that than which nothing greater can be conceived, cannot exist in the understanding alone: then it can be conceived to exist in reality; which is greater.

Therefore, if that than which nothing greater can be conceived, exists in the understanding alone, the very being, than which none greater can be conceived, is one, than which a greater can be conceived. But obviously this is impossible. Hence there is no doubt that there exists a being, than which nothing greater can be conceived, and it exists both in the understanding and in reality.[1]

These are the sentences I am going to explore. And I submit once more that no more splendid headache has ever been composed. Aspirin may help a little, but I want to try something different.

This investigation is extremely complicated. Accordingly, I thought it might be useful to provide a guide concerning what I propose to do. I intend to look closely at the following sentences:

I. "We believe that thou art a being than which none greater can be conceived."

II. "The fool hath said in his heart, there is no God."

III. "This very fool . . . understands what he hears."

IV. "What he understands is in his understanding."

V. "That than which nothing greater can be conceived cannot exist in the understanding alone."

If we look closely at these sentences, we may see how Anselm, as he goes on, gathers in and compounds difficulties. The amazing thing is that out of the confusion woven of fourteen darknesses Anselm should have made one pure ray of light. Such density, and yet such translucence!

I

I want first to discuss the sentence "And, indeed, we believe that thou art a being than which none greater can be conceived." We may notice to

1. Anselm, *Proslogium*, trans. S. N. Deane, 2nd ed. (Chicago: Open Court, 1962), pp. 7–8.

begin with that this sentence, like the other sentences in the discourse, is addressed to God. With this in mind one might consider it strange, as though one intended something like, "We believe it but is it so?" We may, however, discard this as of no particular significance since the address to the deity pertains rather to the form of the meditation. Anselm is musing and Anselm is devout. But the sentence may be troublesome in some other way. The form "We believe" may remind one of the form of the sentences that make up the Apostles' Creed, which begins, "I believe . . . ." They do not, however, go on, "I believe that . . . ." They continue, "I believe in . . . ." "I believe in God, the Father Almighty, Maker . . . ." But we know in any case that Anselm is not, as is the congregation, making a confession of his holy and undoubted Catholic faith. He is not in the church, there are no candles, this is not the hour of prayer. Anselm is sitting at his desk, thinking, writing, trying to get the words in order. In any case the form of these words is not right for the confession. But neither is Anselm meditating out of some Cartesian frame of mind, testing his belief, straining for a doubt to be induced, for a belief shaken. There is no intention to go on, "But may we not be deceived?" When Anselm goes on to ask, "Or is there no such nature?" this is not to be taken as an expression of Anselm's doubt. We know that he had no such doubts. Anselm's question is to be regarded rather as the occasion to present the proof.

And how are we to understand what Anselm is doing? We must remember that Anselm has for a long time been engaged in attempting to devise a proof—neat, clenching, final, clicking—a proof in one quick trick, nothing clumsy, nothing bumbling. And how now would one go about this? Would he borrow a hint from Euclid? Most likely Anselm had no clear idea as to how he would go about this and most likely, too, how he did go about it became clear to him only when he had hit upon the proof itself. At any rate, at some time during his musings the sentence we are busy with occurred to him and we can see how in the sequel it served him. It provided him with a phrase which he employed as something like a definition. I still hesitate to call this a definition since in the sequel it seems to serve rather like a description. In any case my question is as to where Anselm got that phrase, for though Anselm may have been the first to employ it as he did and certainly the first to have written the sentence "We believe that thou art . . .", he may not have invented the phrase itself. This is also apparent in the introductory words "We believe," which suggests that no one would question what follows. The phrase I have in mind is "the being than which none greater can be conceived." It is accordingly from what Anselm treats as common belief that he goes on to lift this phrase. My question can now be restated: Out of what context did Anselm lift that phrase before he incorporated it as a part of the statement of belief? I do not mean that we will discover precisely this phrase in some familiar surroundings, but I do mean that we may discover some phrases enough like this so that we can understand what language is involved here. Once we have discovered this, we can then see the phrase in its natural surroundings, alive and full of joy, and we can also see the same phrase in unnatural surroundings, lifeless and joyless. Later we may see it in the guise of a living thing, together with the help of other illusions providing it the semblance of a moving thing, jerks in an argument.

As you can see, I am taking for granted that the phrase in question (or some phrases very much like it, familiar, breathing, full of spirit) can be found. The reason for this is that I cannot otherwise explain the strong hold this sentence must have had upon Anselm, nor the assent of so many generations of readers of Anselm's proof. The roots of this and of this common assent must lie deep in the language with which Anselm and all these people are so well acquainted. And where now should we look for this? Here again it will be useful to keep in mind that Anselm is a Christian, monk, and archbishop, and that he is busy with a proof for the existence of God. This would certainly involve (proof being what it is) that at the outset he would seek out what to him would seem a clear formulation of the concept God. I do not mean that Anselm would have weighed the matter in this way and considered in some precise fashion what he was about. Nevertheless, I want to suggest that what Anselm is doing may be clearer to us if we think of him as trying to get into perspective the meaning of the word "God" under the special limitation of doing this for a certain purpose. If a definition is required for proof, then that will be the form which the perspective will take. And now where would a Christian look for this? Where but in the Scriptures? Now I do not mean to say that there are any definitions in the Scriptures nor even that Anselm directs his search in this way. He takes what may strike us as a shortcut; namely, to what he regards as a statement of what we Christians all believe. But since we are all Christians and the Bible is our book, this must be where we are led to discover this language. Of course, I do not mean that what Anselm provides as a statement of belief is a statement of belief. It serves Anselm, however, as a sentence holding in perspective some part of the meaning of the word "God," but in such a way as to embody profound confusion and to lead on to even greater densities of the same.

I propose now to go on to find the surroundings of this phrase in several books of the Scriptures, but especially in the Psalms. In this way I expect to exhibit this phrase as a slightly altered fragment of the language of praise. Once this grammatical detail is digested, we may come to see what a surprisingly strange piece of work this argument is. It may help to remark that in the light of this, Anselm's sentence, "We believe that thou art a being than which none greater can be conceived," may be regarded as arising out of a distorted reading of the words of praise. If everything had been kept in order, Anselm might have written, "We all praise thee, O God, at the top of our voices, shouting, Thou art great, O Lord, Our God," but this would have been praise and itself quite useless for his proof. And now I want to pass on to remind us of some of the language of praise after a few introductory remarks about this language.

Praise is common; so is invective. There is fulsome praise, generous praise, hollow praise, insincere praise, half-hearted praise, faint praise. We praise God. We praise men. Sometimes praise is spontaneous. "Bravo! Bravo!" Sometimes we set a time to praise, a special occasion, with a dinner to honor. "Let us now praise famous men." "We come to bury Caesar and not to praise him"; but we praise him all the same. A man may be "damned with faint praise." There is a ceremony of praise; the banner is raised high. So is the football hero he is lifted up. The place of honor is a raised place and the praised sit at the high table. With praise go honor, laurels, decorations, singing telegrams, all hail! And there is singing ("For he's a jolly good fellow"), shouting, blowing of horns, ringing of bells, fireworks, confetti, flowers. With joyful brass sounding and shouting, paper streaming, the gay and loud, the bursting rockets, the umbrella of stars, the glory of the praised is showered upon the blessed. And there is eulogy, the words well spoken, remembering virtues and deeds: they are glorious, and we all join in the exultation. Once they were bigger than man-size, and we'll not forget but praise them. Praise is verve, it is delight, zest, and jubilation. It is the finery of our spirits in noise and color, in the sound of the trumpet and in song, shouting for joy in the blessedness of what is high and noble. Praise is articulate wonder and exultation, a making merry, celebrating the presence or the memory of heroes.

I am sure that I should not have written about praise in this way had I not just lately refreshed myself with the language of praise in the psalms. These writers were, of course, praising God. And what praise it is! Compared to their praise, all other praise is tepid. Here the spirit rejoices. What jubilation and ecstasy! I know of nothing today rivaling this in intensity, that exuberance of the spirit, that extolling of what is high. Here we sing, we praise, we are glad, we bless, we magnify, we exult, we extol, we make a noise, we raise our hands, we dance, we sound the trumpet, we play on the psaltery and harp and with cymbals and dance, with stringed instruments and wind, and organs, and upon the loud cymbals and the high sounding cymbals. What were Bach and Handel doing but praising God?

And now I should like to review some of the language of praise. I have chosen these particular instances as reminders we need in order that we may discover the surroundings of the phrase "the being than which none greater can be conceived." Here are a few:

King Solomon to King Hiram: "And the house which I build is great; *for great is our God above all gods.*"

And here is King David: "Wherefore *thou are great*, O Jehovah God; for there is none like thee, neither is there any God besides thee, according to all that we have heard with our ears." Compare this and the foregoing with Anselm's "Thou are a being than which none greater can be conceived," Anselm gilding the praise of King David.

And here are some sentences from the psalms:

Great is Jehovah and *greatly* to be praised . . . .
Jehovah reigneth; let the people tremble;
He sitteth above the cherubim; (Ps. 48)

Let the earth be moved.
Jehovah is great in Zion. (Ps. 99)

Bless Jehovah, O my soul.
O Jehovah, my God, *thou are very great.* (Ps. 104)

Great is Jehovah and *greatly* to be praised.
And his *greatness* is unsearchable. (Ps. 145)

I have selected these particular cases of the language of praise to stress the role of the word "great" in praise. In the book of Acts it is the Ephesians who cry out, "Great is Diana of the Ephesians." There are also such expressions as "great above all other gods" and "very great" and "great and terrible" and "his greatness is unsearchable." The use of the superlative is common. So we have "neither is there any God beside thee," "a great King above all gods," and so on. And so, too, "a being than which none greater can be conceived."

There are other words which serve in much the same way that the word "great" does. Here, for instance, is the word "high." "It is a good thing to give thanks unto the Lord and to sing praises unto thy name, O most high" (Ps. 92:1). And in the same psalm, "But thou, Lord, art most high forevermore." Here we also have the superlative "most high." Also, "The Lord is high above all nations and his glory above the heavens" (Ps. 113:4). The use of the superlative in praise is common both in Scripture and otherwise: "too wonderful for me," "the peace that passeth understanding," "beyond all estimate," "indescribably lovely," "beyond words," "incomparable," "peerless," "as the heavens are high above the earth, so are my ways higher than your ways, my thoughts than your thoughts," "more than words can tell," "impossibly noble life," "unbelievably fine." By this time it should be unmistakably clear that Anselm's phrase is derived from the language of praise.

Now let us ask: And what would have happened to Anselm's proof if instead of his happening upon the sentence "Thou art a being than which none greater can be conceived," he had happened upon "Thou are a being than which none higher can be conceived," or "none more glorious"? Perhaps it would have made no difference. Here, however, is a sentence from Shakespeare of somewhat the same sort: "O wonderful, wonderful, and most wonderful wonderful; and yet again wonderful . . . ." And now what if Anselm had happened upon "Thou are a being than which none is more wonderful wonderful and yet again more wonderful beyond all that can be conceived"? Would the proof have gone on as in the proof we know? There would perhaps be room for the same misunderstanding.

Let me try once more. The word "Ah!" is certainly an expressive term, expressive of awe and delight, a sort of inarticulate praise. We sometimes ask, "What are you Ah-ing about?" An attentive face and an open mouth go with this. The equivalent of Anselm's sentence will now be something like, "Thou are a being than which none more Ah-ed about or more to be Ah-ed about is conceivable." Ah-ing and praising are human reactions.

There are two further points to be made in connection with the language of praise. First, there are variants of the language of praise that (unlike those mentioned earlier and involving the word "great") would never mislead one in the way in which "God is great" may have done. It is the function of these sentences as expressions of praise which we must keep in mind. One is, "O magnify the Lord with me" (Ps. 34:3). How does one magnify the Lord? By singing out in this way. One may also magnify the Lord by singing out, "Great is Jehovah, our God." Here are others:

> Be thou exalted, Lord. (Ps. 21:13)
> I will extol thee, O Lord. (Ps. 30:1)
> Let the Lord be magnified. (Ps. 35:2)
> Blessed be the Lord God of Israel. (Ps. 41:3)
> O, let the nations be glad and sing for joy. (Ps. 67:6)
> Sing unto God, ye kingdoms. (Ps. 68:32)
> Clap your hands, all ye people. (Ps. 47:1)

The point of introducing these variations of the language of praise is to help us to understand by way of what original misunderstanding Anselm may have gone on with the phrase under investigation as he did. The earlier set of sentences have the form of indicatives—"Great is Jehovah," etc. When removed from their surroundings and cooled for the purpose of proof, they may be mistaken for sentences about God, as though they furnished information or descriptions. But they are no more statements or descriptions than the sentences just quoted. Those by their imperative form prevent at least that misunderstanding. The sentence "Great is our God above all other gods" is not to be mistaken for such a sentence as "High is the Empire State Building above all buildings in New York." Or is it? I'm afraid so.

And now I want to make the second point. We have so far identified the surroundings of that phrase and of similar sentences as psalms but we have not indicated what those surroundings are. The surroundings I am concerned to notice are these: namely, that the psalmist, praising God, remembers what God has done. Here is a nice example from Psalm 103:

> Bless the Lord, O my soul, and all that is within me bless his holy name. Bless the Lord, O my soul, and forget not all his benefits; who forgiveth all thine iniquities; who healeth all thy diseases; who redeemeth thy life from destruc-tion; who crowneth thee with loving kindness and tender mercies; who satis-fieth thy mouth with good things; so that thy youth is renewed like the eagle's, etc.

And here is a part of Psalm 104:

> Bless the Lord, O my soul, O Lord my God, thou are very great; thou are clothed with honor and majesty; who coverest thyself with light as with a garment, who stretchest out the heavens like a curtain; who layeth the beams of

his chambers in the waters; who maketh the clouds his chariots, who walketh
upon the wings of the wind; etc.

These may serve to illustrate the common patterns of the psalm of
praise. There are the commonly introductory sentences of praise and
then continuing in praise, the remembrance of what God has done or
what God does. "Remember his marvelous works that he hath done; his
wonders and the judgments of his mouth . . ." (Ps. 105).

I have now made these rather elaborate explanations of the sentence
"Thou art a Being than which none greater can be conceived" in order
that we might see it in its surroundings, along with the shout and the
joyful noise and the reminders of what God has done. It is to be spoken
in the voice of praise. And the phrase "the being than which none
greater can be conceived" may also be understood in these surroundings. If, however, Anselm first lifts the sentence out of its surroundings
and then goes on to lift the phrase out of the sentence (and we remember
that a sentence or a phrase is to be understood only in its surroundings),
we may anticipate that this is where Anselm's troubles, which do not
seem like troubles, first begin.

And now in the light of all this I should like to return to Anselm's
sentence "We believe that thou art a being than which none greater can
be conceived." And how are we to read this? Why, in the same way in
which we might read, "We believe that we are glad and sing for joy," or,
"We believe that we shout Hallelujah unto thy name," or, "We believe
that we delight in thee, O Lord God of Israel." And need I now add that
this is strange? Surely this is neither praise nor belief but a confusion.

And what in this instance has Anselm done? Clearly, he has lifted
out of the shouting surroundings "with a great shout," a shouting sentence. But now there is no shout. And where is the wonder now, the
delight, and the thanksgiving? Gone with the shout. "We believe that
we thank thee, O Lord." And of course there is no dancing, no clapping
of the hands. And what have the little hills to do with this that otherwise were singing for joy? All that we have now is praise on ice, the
denatured words of praise, dead. And where are those other surroundings, the remembrances of deeds so wonderful, from which the spirit of
praise was transfused? They are all tucked away in the book, forgotten,
irrelevant. And now imagine Anselm. He writes down the sentence
"We believe that thou art a being than which none greater can be conceived." At least that is settled. He looks at it hard or he repeats it to
himself and sees in it now nothing like the climax of acclaim, but a

discovery. So that is what God is. Of all beings conceived and conceivable, none is greater than God. And that is a fact. Praise on ice—some praise, that is—looks like ever so many matters of fact.

No doubt, I have written enough to show what I regard as the confusion involved here, but I have said nothing as to how this same sentence must have struck Anselm nor what might have led to this. Hence, I should like to go on with this.

As far as I know, Anselm provides us with no explanation. Hence, all we can ask is What would a reasonable misunderstanding in this case be? And here the sentence may give us some help. "We believe that thou art a being than which none greater can be conceived" looks like the summary of the results of a series of comparisons. (The expression of praise is nothing of the sort.) There is a building in New York City than which there is none in New York City that is taller. Perhaps there is one on the drawing boards, among the conceivables. But what now are being compared? It seems that *beings* are being compared. But this would, I think, be misleading. We had better say that we are comparing conceivables, and a special class of conceivables; namely, the class of conceivable beings, or rather the class of conceivables, called "beings." But how are we to compare conceivables? We know well enough how to compare horses. There are horse shows and judges of horses at horse shows. Blue ribbons are awarded to the finest horses. There are, no doubt, scores for prance, and scores for stance, and scores for dance, and so on. There are poultry shows, dog shows, cat shows. And at the animal fair there may be a first and grand prize for the finest animal in the fair. This cow is a finer beast than any cat at the fair. For all I know, a tiny white mouse might win the prize; presumably, there is a way of estimating these things. But comparing conceivables cannot be managed in that way. There is no "conceivables fair." Or is there? But it is not simply that conceivable beings are to be compared, for they are also to be arranged in some order of what is called their greatness. Concerning this order, it is said that there is some last conceivable in the order of the progression, beyond which no greater conceivable is conceivable. And that does not mean that some inconceivable does come next.

And if one should ask, "But what are these conceivable beings?" let me suggest that there are conceivables such as "now" and "if" and "one" and "ask" which are certainly conceivable but certainly not as conceivable beings. Some conceivables are beings and some are not. Conceivable beings are "pebbles," "fleas," "stars," etc. In respect to some words, sentences of the form, "It is round," "It is a flea," "It is a pebble," etc., make sense. Each of such sentences is a part of what is meant here by a conceivable of the sort called "beings." If we are satisfied with this, it should speed us on. At least we have enough trouble. In any case I will now hasten to provide a list of conceivable beings, and in the order which some will certainly consider the right order. It will follow more or less the order of evolutionary generation from lesser to greater: a stone, a mite, a horse, a man, Shakespeare, an angel, Satan, Zeus, God. Perhaps it will also now be clear that by a *conceivable* in the case of each of these words, is meant whatever may be said about any stone, any mite, any horse, etc., respectively. So by the conceivable being, "stone," is meant whatever may be intelligibly said about any stone. And now if someone were to say about a stone, that it is a being, not than which none greater can be conceived, but that it is a being than which some being greater than it can be conceived (namely, a mite) perhaps this would be understood. Whatever someone did mean by this, I suppose that he would have to explain this by way of what is said about stones and mites, respectively. I wish that I knew in detail how this explanation would run. It seems that some sort of comparison would be involved upon which one would then say, "And so the mite is higher than the stone." There are shadows here. Albert Schweitzer has reverence for the mite—it is alive—but not for the stone. "Higher" here might then mean no more than that he, Schweitzer, has reverence for the mite but not for the stone. A stone is a stone, but a mite is a mite. The mite is alive, but that the mite is alive must not be regarded as involved in some argument. Nor is it a defense.

Never mind that. If we look upon Anselm's sentence in this way, it must be in the higher reaches of this progression that the main interest lies. Let us suppose that we have gotten on with our conceiving and our comparing of "beings greater than" to Zeus. Zeus is greater than Satan (Is he?) and Satan is greater than the angel Gabriel. (Is that how Milton represents Satan?) And now comes the climax: God is greater than Zeus. At this point the progression ends. Any further conceivable conceived will have to be placed down lower in the order. (It just occurred to me now that there may be some difficulties in this. The conceivable being "God" is defined by what is said of God in the Scriptures—"theology as grammar.") If the place of the conceivable, God, is determined by way of the comparison of what is said of God with what is said of some other conceivables, then the place of the conceivable "God" must await the results of conceiving and further comparisons, and so must remain uncertain. In this way, that God is "the Being than which none greater can be conceived" will itself be no part of what is involved in the conceivable, will be no part of theology. It is then as though Anselm examined "Zeus" and then examined "God" and as a result of this examination Anselm came to make this discovery. This may serve at once to remind us that God is great, and as great as you please is no discovery at all, and that Anselm is mistaking the sentence of praise for that of fact.

It may be interesting in the course of this fantasia of order to notice what determines that Zeus's place is higher than that of Satan. And here is a suggestion. Zeus is quite impressive. He says, "Go to now, ye gods, make trial, that ye may all know. Fasten ye a rope of gold from heaven, and all ye gods lay hold thereof, and all goddesses; yet could ye not drop from heaven Zeus to earth. Zeus, counselor supreme, not though ye toiled sore. But once I likewise were minded to draw with all my heart, then should I draw you up with very earth and sea withal. Thereafter would I bind the rope about a pinnacle of Olympus and so should all those things be hung in air. By so much am I beyond gods and beyond men." And here is another sentence, "And loud as nine thousand men or ten thousand cry in battle when they join the strife of war so mighty was the cry of the strong shaker of the earth sent forth from his heart and great strength he put into the hearts of each of the Achaeans to strive and war unceasingly." Notice that Zeus boasts himself "beyond gods and beyond men." I will not continue the comparison with Satan. Satan, we know, "made himself equal with God" and suffered the consequences. I am introducing the idea of this comparison only in order to try to figure out some more or less plausible misunderstanding of Anselm's sentence.

Suppose now that someone were to remind Anselm of his sentence and of what Zeus could do and were now to put the question "And is not Zeus that being than which none greater can be conceived?" Then how will Anselm answer? He might have quoted a passage from Isaiah, "Therefore the redeemed of the Lord shall return, and come with singing unto Zion; and everlasting joy shall be upon his head; they shall obtain gladness and joy; and sorrow and mourning shall flee away. I, even I, am he that comforteth you; who art thou that thou shouldst be afraid of a man that shall die, and of the son of man which shall be made as grass; and forgettest the Lord, thy Maker, that both stretched forth the heavens and laid the foundation of the earth; and hast feared continually every day because of the fury of the oppressor as if he were ready to destroy? And where is the fury of the oppressor?" And with this, as I am now representing Anselm's hybrid sentence, Anselm (by comparing what is said about Zeus with what is said about God, two conceivables conceived) will have shown himself that God is greater than Zeus.

Perhaps this will be better. Just as there are psalms in the Scriptures praising God, so too there were psalms, or the equivalent, in Hesiod or Homer, praising Zeus. The psalms to Zeus would be composed after much the same fashion as those in the Scriptures: "Great is Zeus, the earth-shaker; Great is Zeus, the cloud-gatherer, etc." Someone familiar with Homer might easily compose such psalms. And now imagine Anselm in Paris reading first some psalms from the Scriptures and then reading some psalms from among the praises of Zeus. Then he would turn to his listeners, "Now which is greater, our God or Zeus?" And all his listeners would reply, "Our God is greater." But what if there were four who replied, "Zeus is greater!" What then? Anselm, presumably, would say that there must be some misunderstanding and he would read the psalms again. And once again they would say, "Zeus is greater!" And Anselm would exclaim, "Is it greater that Zeus should draw up gods and goddesses with the very earth and sea on a rope of gold and hang them all up in air from a pinnacle of Olympus than that God should return the redeemed of the Lord with joy unto Zion and that he should stretch forth the heavens and lay the foundations of the earth?" And they would look puzzled and say that they did not even understand what he was saying. If now Anselm went on insisting that God is not only greater than Zeus but greater than any being conceivable, would not this exhibit a misunderstanding on his part! This suggests questions like, Is the sentence "God created the heavens and the earth" intelligible? Or, How is that sentence to be understood? But the chief lesson once more is that concerning the misleading nature of "greater than." For as it enters into what I regard as a form of misunderstanding, whether it be Anselm's or not, it is treated as though one could show that this or that was greater. It is as though one could compel praise as one can press upon someone a conclusion.

And now I can imagine someone asking, "But why are you making such a fuss about this?" This deserves an explanation.

I was busy with Anselm's first sentence, "We believe that thou art a being than which none greater can be conceived." I tried first of all to exhibit the absurdity of this, the mixture of the grammar of the sentences of praise with that of the grammar of the statement of belief. To Anselm, the sentence obviously seemed far from absurd. It must have seemed to him that what he was saying was beyond all question—which indeed it was—and yet that it made sense to say that we believed it. The question, accordingly, was this: How was Anselm misunderstanding the sentence "Thou art a being than which none greater can be conceived"? That is, by way of what grammatical analogy can we understand what he was doing? And I said that he was regarding this fragment of the language of praise, which is indubitable, which it makes no sense to doubt, as a statement of the results of a comparison. The sentence is similar to sentences which do state such results. Accordingly, this sentence will seem indubitable, and yet, as the statement of the results of a comparison, as subject to error. I tried then to give an account of how one might come to think of this, the comparison of conceivables. It must be remembered that I am not trying to give any account of what Anselm's thoughts were at the time he was writing this piece, nor am I trying to give such an account as Anselm might have given had he come to answer questions. Anselm has himself left us a mere sketch, and that is in part what makes his argument so neat. What I am trying to do is to provide those resources which lie hidden in the background of the language which may help us to see what led Anselm to say what he said. For this purpose I have at times had to engage in fantasy, but this was only in order to get the language into perspective.

But there is one special reason why I have had to elaborate the way in which we might think of Anselm's regarding the sentence "Thou art a being than which none greater can be conceived." I have already referred to this as the reasonable or plausible misunderstanding and I have done this deliberately. For there is another misunderstanding of the same sentence (or a part of it) which enters more directly into the argument, and which I prefer to describe as utterly unreasonable and implausible, explained only by that excess of zeal which Anselm had for proof. I regard it as a plausible misunderstanding that Anselm should have supposed that the discovered God was greater than Zeus by a review of the praises of each. But I regard it as an almost incomprehensible misunderstanding that Anselm should have supposed that in the same way he discovered that God is not a mere idea or an image or a sensation. The explanation for this must wait. Let me suggest this further: the confusion which we meet at the outset I regard as transitional. It is transitional in relation to the other confusion that operates in the argument proper.

II

Now I should like to go on to consider Anselm's reflections on the understanding of the fool. Anselm says, "Or is there no such nature, since 'the fool hath said in his heart, There is no God.'"

The sentence "The fool hath said in his heart, There is no God" interests me not alone because of what Anselm does with it but because a study of the psalm in which it is found, the surroundings of the sentence, reveals something surprising about the meaning of that sentence. And anyone who has a taste for the niceties of language may relish this. Anselm assumes that since "the fool hath said in his heart, There is no God" that "the fool when he hears of this being of which I speak understands what he hears." But the psalm does not support this construction. It does not even support assuming that when the fool hears a psalm intoned that he understands this. If the fool is a Hebrew fool who has as a boy been taught out of the Scriptures and has every year taken his part in the Passover feast and has asked the ceremonial question "What mean ye by this service?" then he would understand a great deal. But even though he did understand the psalms and had once taken part in the singing and been one of the musicians, it would not involve his understanding Anselm's "a being than which none greater can be conceived." Even if we assume the fool understands it, it is clear from the argument that he did not understand it in the same way that Anselm did. And what fools among us understand it? But what I had in mind to point out was that the psalm involves nothing concerning the literacy or illiteracy of the fool. The fool is an unrighteous man. And when the psalmist writes that "the fool hath said in his heart," this is not to be understood as meaning that the fool said this to himself, nor that when he is asked what he has said in his heart that this would mean anything to him or that he could tell. It is the speaking of his misdeeds which is the saying in his heart. He utters misdeeds and they are speeches out of the fullness or the emptiness of his heart. Actions speak neither Hebrew nor English. There is a version here of "By their fruits ye shall know them." So the fool's deeds show, not that he is saying to himself, "There is no God," but that he does not believe, that he neither keeps God's commandments nor fears God.

The psalm begins with the line already quoted, "The fool hath said . . . ." But it goes on, "They are corrupt, they have done abominable works, there is none that doeth good," and it continues, "They are all gone aside, they are altogether become filthy," they "eat up my people as they eat bread." I am emphasizing this detail in order to point out another instance of Anselm's lifting out of its surroundings a sentence which in these surroundings has a use which is quite different from that to which Anselm now adapts it. In this case it may not make much difference since there are also fools who noisily proclaim, "There is no

God," others who mutter this to themselves hiding their unbelief, and still others whose deeds speak—perhaps even such deeds as contradict their mouths. Anselm's fool is a literate fool, but he is not the fool of this psalm.

Let us then consider: There is a fool and he said, "There is no God." Anselm tells us nothing about this fool, what the occasion was on which he said this, what troubles he had had, etc. We cannot even tell from what Anselm says whether it is precisely the fool's saying this that makes him a fool. "The fool" in this case is a barren concept. So we will have to make up our own fool. These necessities are laid upon us by our working with a mere sketch. Concerning this fool, Anselm does not tell us merely that he understands what he is saying when he says, "There is no God," but that "this very fool when he hears of this being of which I speak—a being than which none greater can be conceived—understands what he hears, and what he hears is in his understanding." I want to try to get this in perspective.

Let us suppose that this fool is a renegade Jew and the time is that of the captivity. He remembers well how it was at home when he was a boy and at his grandfather's house, the reading of the book, his grandfather poring over the Talmud, the candles in the house, the feast of lights, the unleavened bread, and the Sabbaths when no servant worked and no ox and no ass pulled anything. He remembers, too, as a boy hearing the choirs intoning psalms in the congregation, the same choirs intoning now their disenchanted hopes. It is all very sad now. He sees the foreign soldiers in the streets and thinks of other days when his father walked so proudly. Times have changed; it has been very hard. His grandfather has been dead now a long time, his father and mother are gone, and the family has been scattered so he never sees them any more. Among his own people he has few friends and most of them, too, have departed from the old ways. Abraham, Isaac, and Jacob, and Samuel, Joshua, and Moses, and Saul, David and Solomon—these names still bring tears to his eyes. "They are my people." A man is not a stone. But the God of Abraham, Isaac, and Jacob? There is still a congregation in the town, men of faithful memory who are diligent each Sabbath day, keeping themselves and the Sabbath holy. Sometimes he stands at the door where they meet and he listens to the reading, those stirring and terrible chapters from Exodus and Deuteronomy, and he hears the injunction, "Only take heed to thyself, and keep thy soul diligently, lest thou forget the things which thine eyes have seen and lest they depart from thy heart all the days of thy life; teach them to thy sons and thy sons' sons."

And he hears again of "the mountain that burned with fire" and of "the darkness, clouds, and thick darkness" and of "his voice out of the midst of the fire." He is distressed, both sad and angry. He has neither sons nor sons' sons, and if he did, what would he teach them? He no longer believes. He is desolate, tender with memories, but without hope. God, too, is only a memory. And when he hears the psalm "Bless the Lord, O my soul, and all that is within me bless his holy name. Bless the Lord, O my soul, and forget not all his benefits," he stands grim at the door, looking in upon those old men in their little black caps. But he does not enter. He turns and walks hurriedly away.

III—IV

I have now presented to you Anselm's fool. He has heard the words of Moses, the words that once made him fear, and the words of the psalm once heard in blessing and still sweet to his ear. Of this fool Anselm says, "This very fool when he hears . . . understands what he hears. . . ." And surely Anselm is right about that since that is just the sort of fool I have presented. How could he not understand seeing he was brought up as he was. Anselm continues, "Understands what he hears and what he understands is in his understanding; although he does not understand it to exist." And now what are we to make of this?

The fool stood at the door and he heard the words of the chapter from Deuteronomy and the words of the psalm, and he understood those words. He was moved by them, attracted and repelled. Wistful he listened; and yet when the injunctions were sounded, "Hearken," and, "Keep therefore and do them," "Take heed to thyself and keep thy soul diligently," "Take heed unto yourselves, lest ye forget," and when he heard the pleadings and the wooings and the threatenings, he neither hearkened nor heeded nor feared. Yet he knew well enough how those pious old men with their long beards received those words and how they kept them in their hearts and how those words ruled them and how they raised their spirits and comforted them as a refuge in their calamities. But when they invited him in to join them in remembering, in prayer, in praise, he shook his head and would not, could not. God to heed, to obey, to fear, to remember, to hearken to! What is God? "A shout in the street." And he turned away, miserable, guilty, numb. A man now turning against his youth! And had he not for years heard those words, and been taught, and taken his part at the feasts and the commemorations? The shout of Abraham, Isaac, and Jacob!

The question is as to what Anselm means by saying that the fool understands what he hears. But first let us take notice. The men in the congregation might be said to understand in a way in which the fool does not. They remember what God has done; they receive and obey the commands as God's commands; they heed and fear God; they praise God and they pray; they also bring their offerings. He, the fool, does not and cannot do any of these things. And yet he understands what they are doing, remembering, heeding, obeying, fearing, praising, and praying. Apart from his once having taken part in all of these, these have their analogues in human relationships. All these people in the congregation are like people who are devoted to an unseen king, a government in exile or in their exile, and the fool understands that. But the fool has said in his heart and at the door, "The King is dead."

So Anselm says that the fool "understands what he hears." And I suppose that if we asked him how he knows this, he might explain in the way in which I have already indicated we might. "Of course, of course, the fool understands. Wasn't he brought up to understand?" and so on. But now the language begins to thicken. "The fool . . . understands what he hears and what he understands is in his understanding." Let us now first ask whether when Anselm noticed that the fool "understands what he hears" he also noticed that the fool had something in his understanding and it turned out to be what he understands? Did Anselm look twice—once to find that the fool understood, and then once more to discover what was in the fool's understanding? We will not attempt any answer to this question. Instead, let us see whether we can figure out just what it is that is said to be in the fool's understanding. Consider then that the fool understands the words:

Great is Jehovah and greatly to the praised.
And his greatness is unsearchable.
Thou art a being than which none greater is conceivable,
O Lord.

He hears these words and he understands them. What he understands is in his understanding and it is the words he understands. So the words are in his understanding. This may seem to be all right, but it is nevertheless wrong, even if the words are in his understanding. Where are the words? They are in the book, in the mouth of the reader, and the fool might have stored the words in his memory. All the same, Anselm was not speaking of the words even though it is words the fool understood and what he understood was in his understanding. How do I know? Well, Anselm goes on to say, "Although he does not understand it to exist." It seems obvious that if we asked the fool (who understands what he hears) whether what he hears is in his understanding, he would not say that what he hears does not exist. He is not that sort of fool. He has heard the words written above and so has everyone else. But what then? Well, what else is there? There is the meaning of the words, of course. If the fool has heard those words and understood them, then he may, for instance, be able to explain how he understands these words and what he then explains is the meaning. You cannot explain the meaning of a word or words unless there is the meaning of the words, and where would the meaning be but in the understanding? What does a man do who explains the meaning but doesn't tell you about what he has there? So when a man understands the words, obviously there are words that may be on the page, but there is also the meaning of the words, which is certainly not on the page. "Here the words, there the meaning." Where now? In the understanding. The meanings must be accessible and convenient to anyone who is to explain them. I do not suppose the meanings need to be there all the time even when the words are far away or nowhere in sight or hearing. But they must be there when you understand the words. This seems to be undeniable unless one intended to say that they might be in some place, also readily accessible, but not in the understanding. Still the understanding seems as good a place as any.

In the quotation above, beginning, "Great is Jehovah," there are some twenty or more words and each has a meaning. And when the fool hears these words and understands them, there are twenty or more meanings of those words in the fool's understanding. There is nothing startling about this, and I had no intention of surprising anyone with this. What I wanted to point out is that there are words and meanings here in which Anselm has no interest at the moment. And if we had selected some other portion of Scripture that the fool also understands, this would be clearer still. He would, for instance, not be interested in saying that the meaning of the word "sons" or "mountain" or "darkness" or "cloud" is in the fool's understanding. If now we remember that the fool said, "There is no God," then we may realize that what Anselm meant to say was that when the fool hears the word "God," or "Jehovah," or "Lord," then the meaning of these words is in his understanding. This may help to explain how Anselm goes on, as he does, to say, "Although he does not understand it to exist." This may still strike one as strange since what the fool presumably does not understand is that the meaning of the word "God"—which he understands, and which he has in his understanding—still does not exist. There is the word "God" and there is the meaning of the word "God." There is also something which Anselm refers to as "it." Now what could that be? It seems preposterous to think of the fool as one who understands the word "God," and yet when you ask him whether he understands the word he says that the word has no meaning; that is, that "it" does not exist. So once more, what is "it"?

Before going on with this I want to say something about the meaning of the word "God." Anselm is a Christian, and accordingly, when he is busy with the meaning of the word "God," the meaning with which he is concerned must be regarded then as Christian; namely, that embodied in the Scriptures—"theology as grammar." The Scriptures are also described as "the word of God" and accepted by Christians as a revelation. Here God declares himself to men and reveals his love towards men, seeking to draw them unto himself. There is great variety in the ways in which God has pursued these purposes, as the variety of forms and style in the books of the Bible makes plain. This is the role of the Scriptures as a sacred book. But there is something else pertinent to our present investigation. If anyone is interested in getting into perspective the meaning of the word "God" among Christians, his resource must be the Scriptures. Anyone who in Anselm's time or our time understands the word "God" will know what sentences involving this word make sense and which do not make sense and he will in this have been guided by and nurtured in the language of the Scriptures. Generally, this will involve religious education both in literature and in practice—singing, ritual, sermons, sacraments, feasts, etc. Accordingly, if the fool understands what he hears, as a Jew or as a Christian, this will involve that he, having been brought up in the Jewish or the Christian religion will be able to distinguish between sense and non-sense in respect to what people say and do employing that word. Heresy is Christian or Jewish non-sense. And now the point of what I am saying is that to understand a word is to have an ability, the ability to speak and to write the language in which that word occurs, and to understand others who speak and write. The understanding of a Christian consists in his ability to employ the word "God" in his Christian practice, in prayer, in praise, etc. And the fool? He has no more than the ability to distinguish sense and non-sense when he stands at the door and hears. He knows the Scriptures, too, and listens with understanding. But he neither remembers, as those do who are inside, nor does he praise God, nor pray, nor confess, nor offer gifts. He can also explain to others.

Now let us return to Anselm. Anselm said that the fool understands what he hears. He adds that what the fool understands is in his understanding. The fool has the meaning and he grasped it. And that is what is in his understanding. But if we now mean (when we say that the fool understands) that he is scripturally literate, that he has a certain ability with respect to that language, that he is able to do so and so, then it seems that Anselm has said something like what he might say of a man who could lift heavy weights; namely, that he had lifting weights in his arm. This might be picturesque language, but it would be a mistake if one expected to find anything but muscles, etc., in the strong man's arm. Accordingly, it now seems that if Anselm intended to explain to us what he meant by saying that the fool understands what he hears, he might better have told us that the fool can (in respect to the words he has heard) tell us what in the service led up to their speaking these words, what special circumstances are involved as in the case of the Passover Feast, what the attitudes of the people in the congregation were (kneeling, bowing their heads, or raising their hands), and what came after—language has surroundings. But once again, if Anselm had said this, then the addition "although he did not understand it to exist" would be incomprehensible. There certainly is no reason for supposing that the fool would deny that he could give these explanations.

We should now be in a position to understand what has led Anselm to say what he says. The fool understands the words he hears, so he is doing two things. He hears the words and he understands. Hearing and understanding are different, but now as the words are to the hearing, so the meaning is to the understanding. Understanding might be thought of as a special internal form of hearing. And now what could the meaning be? Well, in the case of the word "God," however it may be with other words, the answer is clear. The meaning of the word "God" must be what the word names, so God is the meaning of the word "God." Perhaps we can also see how Anselm regarded the state of the fool's understanding. The fool understands the word "God," and so he must have something in his understanding. The fool does not deny that he has something in his understanding. Since he is Anselm's fool, he may agree with Anselm that if he understands a word, then the meaning of that word must be in his understanding, and it must be what the word is a name of. So too with the word "God." But there are now apparently two sorts of things which bear the names which are words one understands. One says of things of the one sort, that they do not exist; of the other sort, one says that they do exist. The fool, accordingly, has in his mind the meaning of the word "God," it bears that name, but he classifies it wrong. He says that it belongs to the class of those things in his understanding which do not exist. Anselm tells us nothing about how either the fool or Anselm manages to make this distinction, nor how the fool ever came to make this mistake.

There is something very important here for this discussion. In connection with such expressions as "the abominable snowman" and "the monster of Loch Ness" and "the suspected murderer of the man who died in a fall" and "ghosts" and "whooping cranes" and "passenger pigeons" and "the inhabitants of Easter Island" and "descendants of Julius Caesar" (each of which is a "name" and has a meaning), one might make a classification. There would be those of which one might then say that they exist and those of which one might say that they do not exist. In connection with this one could also go on to indicate by what sorts of investigations one came to make these distinctions. If then the meaning of the words "exists" and "does not exist" are to be understood in just such surroundings, the question arises as to how we are to understand not only Anselm (who says that God exists), but also the fool (who "does not understand it to exist"). If the fool should explain this latter by saying that he does not understand what Anselm is saying when he says that God exists, since the word "exists" has the surroundings of "the abominable snowman" and "ghosts" and "whooping cranes," etc., then he would seem to have the advantage. It may be well here to remember that the fool of the psalm makes no such classification as is attributed to the fool of Anselm's argument. It is his deeds that utter his unbelief. He is not represented as making a mistake in sorting out his ideas.

v

We are now at this point. The fool has something in his understanding called "God." He classifies it as belonging to the class of things that do not exist. Anselm is now ready to correct him. In this case, whatever the fool may do in the case of "whooping cranes," all he needs to do now is examine what he has in mind, or should I say examine the name? With Anselm's help he is to substitute for the word "God" the expression which Anselm lifted from the psalms, namely, "the being than which none greater can be conceived." Once he does this he will reclassify what he has in his understanding. That is, he will see at once that "the being than which none greater can be conceived" exists.

Presumably, this will help the fool only if he understands this expression. Does he understand it? Of course. He has understood it all along and also when he stood at the door of the meeting place. He understood it then as a slightly mutilated fragment of the language of praise. It is among the sentences like, "Bless the Lord, O my soul." So he understands it all right even though he never pours out his soul in blessing. Let us see what this comes to. Suppose that the fool recites Psalm 145 for Anselm. It begins, "I will extol thee, my God, O King"; and then are the lines, "Great is Jehovah, and greatly to be praised." The psalm continues with the praises of God's mercies and of his "wondrous works." So he certainly knows what the surroundings of this phrase of Anselm's are. His understanding before did not incline him to join the congregation then, and to be reminded of it now does not either. The difficulty obviously arises out of his not sharing Anselm's misunderstanding. Let us see how this goes.

The fool has the meaning of the word "God" in his understanding. But the fool does not realize what it is he has there. So Anselm tells him that he has a being there, "the being than which none greater can be conceived." Now the words of praise are going about in the guise of a description. We have earlier seen out of what more or less plausible comparison this illusion might arise. But we have now introduced them into a situation in which this plausible comparison will be of no use. For how would the fool be moved from his position, change the classification, by reminding him of other greatness, the praises of Shakespeare and Milton's Satan and Zeus? Praise is praise, but that does not mean you will find Zeus on Olympus.

Now I want to return to Anselm's words: "Hence even the fool is convinced that something exists in the understanding, at least, than which nothing greater can be conceived. . . . And assuredly that than which nothing greater can be conceived cannot exist in the understanding alone. For suppose it exists in the understanding alone: then it can be conceived to exist in reality; which is greater." Here again we meet that previously noticed classification. There are, first of all, existences in the understanding. We have already noticed some instances of these. And now there are the two subclasses, those which exist in the understanding alone, and those which exist in the understanding and also in reality. But how are we to think of "existences in the understanding alone"?

Shall we suggest that this must be done by introspection? Think of the abominable snowman, which you most likely think does not exist anyhow, and then see what the existence in your understanding is like. He is a very large creature, half bear and two-thirds man, who walks on four feet that leave the footprints of only two, who eats storms and is always seen disappearing. Let me suggest then that an existence in the understanding alone is a mere idea and a mere idea is an image. Perhaps we could say that a sensation, too, is an existence in the understanding alone. Now then we might explain the classification in this way: There is a class composed of images and sensations. Sensations clearly exist in the understanding alone. There are no sensations in the sky nor in a stone. I am now inclined to say that images, too, exist only in the understanding. Where else could images exist? And yet one gets the impression that many of these existences in the understanding exist also in reality. And so it would seem that these existences in the understanding are not images. What now could exist both in the understanding and in reality? Why, a universal. Might not a universal exist in the image which exists in the understanding, and also in the cat on the fence which is in no one's understanding, but in reality?

I asked what sort of something this is in the fool's understanding. And I should like to remind you that the question is misleading. I was inclined to say that the fool has a grammatical mistake in his understanding, but that would not be quite right. The whole phrase "something in his understanding" is a grammatical mistake. Accordingly, our question should be, What sort of grammatical mistake is this? This now is a partial description: Anselm is thinking of the meaning of an expression, the function of that expression as a thing, and of the understanding as a place, and accordingly we get "something in the understanding." Now superimposed is another confusion, a difference in somethings in the understandings (meanings); namely, the difference between somethings that "exist in the understanding alone" and somethings that "exist both in the understanding and in reality," perhaps, the difference in the meaning between such expressions as "the abominable snowman" and "ghosts" and the meaning of such expressions as "horses" and "cows." Now comes the question What sort of something is this—what sort of meaning is this—that the word "God" has? Since the fool has this something (meaning) in his understanding, the question is now understood in this way: Is the word "God" a word with the meaning such as that of such words as "abominable snowman" and "ghosts," or such as that of such words as "horses" and "cows"? Regarded in this way, the fool says that it has a meaning, a kind of something, such as the expression "abominable snowman" has; but Anselm says that it has a meaning, a king of something, such as the word "horses" has. And it is this that Anselm proves.

Now notice: If we say that the meaning (the something) of the expression "abominable snowman" exists in the understanding alone, we might think of this as an image. Images exist in the understanding alone. If Anselm should ask himself what the meaning of that expression is, he would look into his understanding and find the something; namely, the image of the snowman. But if we went to the Himalayas to look for the meaning of the expression, he would not find it. So the meaning of that expression exists only in his understanding. And what now about the meaning of the word "horse"? Well, again, he looks into his understanding, and there it is—the image of a horse. And does it exist in the understanding alone? No indeed; he went out into the stable and there he found the meaning of the word "horse" eating oats. So the meaning of the word "horse" exists not only in the understanding but also in the stable. This is one way of understanding Anselm, and I do not know a better way of understanding Anselm's misunderstanding.

And now we also have a way of understanding Anselm's misunderstanding of the fool. The fool understands the word "God." He looks into his understanding and then he finds the meaning of the word "God." Will it do to say that the meaning of the word "God" is an image? At any rate it is a something. Now the fool asks himself, "Is the meaning of the word 'God' in my understanding alone?" and he decides to find out. He visits the Himalayas, he goes to the stable, he scans the heavens with a telescope. He cannot find the meaning of the word "God" anywhere but in his understanding. So he concludes that the meaning, "the something" of the word "God" exists only in his understanding. Now notice that Anselm does not say, "But you have not looked in the uttermost parts of the sea," or "east of the sun and west of the moon." Such investigations would in any case be too tedious for Anselm. Anselm needs something quick as lightning. And so we get the proof. With this, I want to add, he also abandons the surroundings of the word "exists."

Notice now the proof. I said that the fool understands the word "God," but he says that the meaning of the word "God" exists only in his understanding. Anselm induces him to substitute for the word "God," "a being than which none greater can be conceived." It is not clear to me how this is done, whether Anselm intends that these expressions mean the same or whether the latter is intended only to describe the something in the fool's understanding called "God." I think it must be the latter. This introduces a new confusion. There is first something, namely, the meaning of the word "God," so we describe it. What we actually have are two expressions—the word "God" and the expression "a being than which none greater can be conceived." The meaning of these expressions is related, for instance, in the Psalms. But the meaning of the latter is not to be regarded as a description of the meaning of the former. It is simply that in praise of God men may employ the latter.

By way of compounding confusions we have arrived at this: that the fool has in his understanding something; namely, a being than which none greater can be conceived. Now the question is as to whether a being than which none greater can be conceived *can* exist only in the understanding. It is obvious that the abominable snowman, I mean the something which is the meaning of that expression, *can* exist only in the understanding. But then no one ever said of it that it was a being than which none greater can be conceived. If anyone ever did say that about the something in the understanding (which is the meaning of the expression "the abominable snowman"), then, of course, he would no longer say that it could exist only in the understanding. It simply cannot. That would follow in this way: If I say that anything, snowman or God, is a being than which none greater can be conceived, I mean that it cannot exist in the understanding alone but must exist both in and out of the understanding. Suppose that Anselm would explain this sentence in this way: If I say that anything, snowman or God, is a being than which none greater can be conceived, then it will certainly be preposterous of anyone to ask me whether what I am so excited about is just in my understanding. If the fool were given the first explanation, he would simply have to deny that he meant anything of the sort by "God is a being than which none greater can be conceived," which is obvious enough, too, since he already said that this something exists in the understanding alone. And if you ask him what he did mean, he might refer you to Psalm 103. There you will find the being than which none greater can be conceived, and it exists in my understanding and in other understandings perhaps, but in understandings alone. And if Anselm urges upon him the second explanation, then he may say that if there are people who are so excited about what they have in their understanding then it may be preposterous for them to say that it exists only in their understandings, but that he is not that excited, which once again is shown by the fact that he still says that the something exists only in his understanding.

This is the intelligible basis of Anselm's argument. There is a man also called a fool who stands at the door of the meeting place and hears the Scriptures read. He understands it but he pays no heed. He says, as it were, "There is no God." He goes home and about his business. Perhaps in another year he will return to hear the reading again. Out of this simple situation and what I venture to call a magic formula, Anselm manages to fashion a proof.

Now, let us see what Anselm does. Anselm notices that the fool stands at the door and hears what is read and that he understands. So far it is the same as in the other case. But now we have an addition. He sees that the fool has something in his understanding. He asks the fool, "What is that you have in your understanding?" The fool falls in with this and says, "O, nothing, just something in my understanding." Anselm recognizes this as a mistake and goes on. "You have Godot in your understanding, don't you?" And the fool says, "Yes." "Well," continues Anselm, "if you describe Godot as Godot who cannot be just something in your understanding, then you will see that you made a mistake when you said, 'O, nothing, just something in my understanding.'" "But," asks the fool, "why should I describe Godot in this way?" And now Anselm says, "Because, as you know, all the people praise him so. They cry out to Godot, 'Thou art a being than which none greater can be conceived.' So that's what you have in your understanding." To which the fool replies, "And so that's it. I have something in my understanding and all the people shout about it and say that it is not something just in my understanding. But what has their praising it and saying this got to do with my saying that it is not just something in my understanding? Let us put it this way: I have something in my understanding. People ask me what it is and I say, 'O, nothing, just something in my understanding.' But other people when they hear the word which occasions my having something in my understanding when I say this, do not say this. I ask one of them, 'What do you have in your understanding?' And he begins praising it. And when I go on, 'And is it just in your understanding?' he says, 'What do you think I am, a fool?' and he goes on with his praises. But it doesn't lead me to praise anything. And when people now ask me, 'What do you have in your understanding?' I say as I said before, 'O, nothing, just something in my understanding.' If someone asks, 'But haven't you heard?' I say, 'Yes, yes, I've heard everything. What others say and do, hearing what I hear, doesn't affect me. I'm a decent citizen.

But I don't sing praises to what I have in my understanding. I'm a plain unbeliever. I'm not even waiting for Godot.' "

In order to make up this conversation I have had to get the fool to enter into the confusion concerning something just in his understanding. But I have permitted him freedom from the confusion concerning the language of praise.

I am not getting along very well with this, but perhaps I have given it up anyhow. I do want to take one more look at "he has something in his understanding but he doesn't know what it is." (He says that it is in his understanding alone, but that is not so.) What is the analogy here? A man walks with a limp. Someone asks, "You have something in your knee?" The man replies, "Yes, something in my knee." The other asks, "And what is it?" And the reply is, "O, just something in my knee." The conversation goes on, "Just something in your knee? Not a bone, for instance." The man smiles, "O, no. I mean a pain. If you have a pain in your knee, and if it's in your knee, it can't be anywhere else. If it were somewhere else, it wouldn't be the pain in your knee. So I said it was just in my knee."

"But aren't you making a mistake? Let me examine your knee." And he pulls a needle out of the man's knee. "See," he says, "you were wrong. It wasn't just in your knee after all since I've pulled it out." The man is flabbergasted. "And I was sure I had a pain in my knee and it's turned out not to be a pain at all but a needle. How could I have made such a mistake?" Anselm now explains, "I said you have something in your knee greater than which none is conceivable, so you might have known it wasn't a pain, seeing ever so many things conceivable—such as a needle or water—are greater than a pain. Anything which is just something in a knee, like a pain, is obviously not as great as something which can be not only in a knee but which can also be drawn out of a knee—'which is greater.' "

I was pretty sure I would not be able to do it.

The common form of the psalm of praise in which there may be something misleading is this: there are the introductory sentences of praise, and then follow the remembering of the wondrous works. The introductory words are like a fanfare, the great shout; there is no logical connection. One would be misled if he thought that from the introductory words of praise he could now go on to infer that God must have done so-and-so, or that the introductory words were a summary and whatever there was summarized could be inferred. The summary, then, the words or sentences of praise, would be an abbreviation of what followed in greater detail. This is a mistake. The psalm contains no argument and no conclusions. One praises, remembering. One shouts the sentences of praise and then goes on remembering, praising. But in his argument Anselm treats the introductory sentence of praise either as a sentence from which one can infer what God is being praised for, or (as I suggested) a summary. But one might then more reasonably suppose that one could infer all the rest of the psalm from the introductory words of the psalm. This would save one's remembering. But actually nothing can be inferred. If one is acquainted with the form of the psalm, then if one hears someone or a group, in the service, beginning with the introductory words of the psalm, then one may know how they will go on, since one knows the psalm. This is rather like knowing the form of a sonnet. It may be that the [logical] form—"Because . . ." and "For . . ."—is what misleads in this case. It is certainly clear that in his argument Anselm is misconstruing the words of praise by trying to deduce from the sentence "Thou art a being than which none greater can be conceived" what he must have regarded as a necessary part of the reason for saying this. But there is no such necessary reason and no reason at all. In the psalm there are no reasons even if one might give as a reason some part of what is in the psalm if one were called upon to justify one's praise. But the remembering is not a justification. The remembering is praise.

Anselm's proof is sometimes formulated in this way. "I have the idea of a most perfect being, and if I have the idea of a most perfect being, then implied in this is the idea that the most perfect being exists." Now what are we to say about this? To have the idea of the most perfect being is to understand this expression "the most perfect being." If someone understood this, he also would be able to identify the most perfect being if it were offered. So, if someone pointed to a stone and asked, "Is this it?" the person who understood this expression would be able now to say whether it was or not. Let us suppose that he would say, "No." Then other things would be pointed to and the same answer would be made, "No, that's not it." That he understood it would not in the least involve that at some time someone would point to something and that he would then say, "Yes, that's it." All that would be involved is that if it ever were presented, he would be able to identify it. But his now being able to do this would not involve that it is available for this.

In general it is a part of the grammar of ever so many concepts that so-and-so or a so-and-so exists. If one understands the concept, then one understands also so-and-so exists. Consider the expression "most

perfect woman" or "most perfect man." Let us suppose that these expressions have a meaning and that someone understands them. With
some experience now he might say, "There is no such being as the
most perfect woman or the perfect woman. There is no perfect woman.
Any woman has some defect, a mole, for instance, or a sharp tongue, or
a clumsy thumb." But there is provision for "The most perfect woman
exists." You may say, "I have found her."

On this account of the matter the mistake lies in mistaking one's
ability to identify the most perfect being for one's saying that the most
perfect being exists, mistaking this grammatical feature of the word for
an assertion.

But the primary mistake is to assume that the sentence "God exists" is a part of the grammar of the word "God." That Anselm should
attempt to prove this makes it appear that it does come in somewhere,
apart from the proof itself. But where then?

"I have the idea of a most perfect being."

"Well, what is it?"

Then he tells you; he quotes Psalm 103. What better, indeed, could
he do? So that is his idea. Let us suppose he quotes it as what the
psalmist sings. Then you ask him, "And has he forgiven your iniquities? And has he healed your diseases?" And he smiles, and says,
"My iniquities, what are they? And as for my indigestion I take Tums,
which quiets my complaining."

I want once again to try to review. The sentence of praise is, "Thou
art a being than which none greater can be conceived." Now Anselm,
overhearing some worshipper in the temple, beginning this psalm, and
realizing that this is the man Reuben, a righteous man, says to himself,
"Now there is a man who believes and who remembers day by day
what God has done, that he has made the world in six days and that the
heavens declare his glory, and what he has done for his people and
what in particular he has done for Reuben." Anselm could do this only
if he knew the form of the psalm.

Now consider the case as Anselm thinks of it.

There is the fool, and not a devout man at all. He mutters to himself, "Thou art a being than which none greater can be conceived," but
he is not in prayer. He is not addressing God. He never prays. He says
this and frowns. Perhaps he says, "Bah!" Now Anselm overhears him.
It is clear enough to Anselm that the fool is a fool. And so, though he
may allow that the fool understands these words—otherwise why does
he frown so?—Anselm cannot now infer that the fool, like Reuben,

believes and remembers day by day what God has done, and so on. He neither believes nor remembers, and, of course, if he does not believe, what should he remember? All the same, Anselm makes a point of saying that the fool understands the sentence he repeated, which may well be. And now what would it be like for the fool to understand this sentence? Well, why should he not understand it in the same way that Anselm himself understood it when he heard Reuben, the righteous man, intone with reverent attitude those same words in the temple. The fool might also make a comment about Reuben, the righteous man, who believes and remembers what God has done. The fool could not do this, of course, if he were not acquainted with the psalms, the psalms of praise. Naturally, there is a difference in the way in which Anselm listens to Reuben, taking it all in reverently just as Reuben himself engages in the psalm, itself praising. In this case too the fool hears, and shakes his head, and frowns. Here, then we have a clear case of what one would mean by saying that the fool understood the sentence which he repeated and which he overheard as he passed the door of the temple.

But this is not at all how Anselm goes on to write of the fool's understanding that sentence. Whereas I have tried to present the meaning of that sentence by way of the surroundings of that sentence in the life of the psalmist who utters it, Anselm looks at meaning, and in this instance, at the meaning of the phrase "a being than which none greater can be conceived" in an obviously different way. If the fool understands that phrase then there must be something, namely, the meaning of that phrase in the fool's understanding. So far as I can make out, he thinks of that phrase as a description of the something in the fool's understanding. I take it that the movement of the proof depends upon this way of regarding the phrase, in the first place as a description, and of understanding as a having in the understanding the something which is described by that phrase. The rest is a matter of figuring out the meaning of that phrase which then the fool does not understand. It comes to this, then: that the fool who is said to understand this phrase and has the meaning, the something, in his understanding, still does not understand what it is he has in his understanding. It seems, accordingly, that the fool understands the phrase sufficiently so that the something is in his understanding but not sufficiently so that he also realizes what the something is that he has in his understanding. It is almost as though he had not examined closely what he has there. But at the same time he cannot examine what he has there without the help of the phrase whose meaning that something is.

Now notice how Anselm goes on. The fool admits that he has something in his understanding and, of course, that it is "the being than which none greater can be conceived." But now he is represented as saying that it exists in his understanding alone. Let us see what contrast is involved here. The fool, of course, could have gone on repeating to himself the whole of the psalm which he heard Reuben, the righteous man, intone in the temple. When Reuben does this, Reuben is praising God, as we have seen. And what is the fool doing? Well, we might say that the fool is ridiculing Reuben or that he is gnashing his teeth, showing his displeasure or expressing his displeasure at the thought of Reuben or of any man praising God for making such a world and such people in it. In any case, there is nothing for the fool to react to or against but people like Reuben. Only in this way can we see the fool alive. Has there ever been a fool who said, "I understand the phrase 'the being than which none greater can be conceived' and so I have in my understanding the something which is that being, but it exists in my understanding alone?"

Consider in any case how we might think of this. The fool says, "The being than which none greater can be conceived exists in my understanding alone." Now Anselm asks, "And what being is this?" To this the fool replies, "The being who made the world in six days and rested on the seventh day, the being who called Abraham out of Ur of the Chaldees, who saved believing Noah and his family from the flood, who led the people of Israel out of Egypt, who keepeth Israel, who forgiveth our iniquities, who healeth all our diseases, and so on." The fool gives Anselm the rigmarole. And now Anselm asks, "And that being exists only in your understanding?" to which the fool replies, "Of course." And now how is Anselm to go on? He might have gone on, "Surely God is great, and greatly to be praised for his mighty works. And the psalmists have sung God's praises for having done all these things. But haven't you forgotten something?" To which the fool responds, "Well, what?" And now Anselm says, "Haven't you forgotten that that being exists in your understanding? Isn't that wonderful?" Now the fool grows impatient. "I thought you were asking me what being this is that I have in my understanding and now you expect me to add among other things that the being in my understanding is in my understanding? In any case I do not think of the being in my understanding as somehow to be rejoiced at because that being graciously consented to come into my understanding from outside my understanding. There is in any case nothing in my understanding but the meaning of all those sentences I recited to you."

Let me try to see through this. The meaning of the word "God" is seen in perspective in the language of the Scriptures. If the fool is literate he may be able to recite the relevant passages. If now Anselm had asked, "And do you pray to God? Do you fear God? Do you believe in God?" the answer might have been, "No. There is no God." But this must not be taken as a reaction to God. It is a reaction to men who do believe. But Anselm is treating "There is no God" as though this were a reaction to God himself. This is what comes of treating the meaning of the phrase as though this were a something in the understanding, God is the understanding.

"As great as can be conceived."
"Greater than which none can be conceived."
"Greater than which none can be in the understanding alone."

Where are concepts? In the understanding alone. So we have a concept than which no greater concept can be conceived, or can be in the understanding alone.

The difference between "I see it" and "I imagine it." So try to imagine God.

Notes on Kierkegaard's
"The Monstrous Illusion"

Most of this paper was delivered as the Willis M. Tate-Willson Lecture at Southern Methodist University in October 1970, under the auspices of the Graduate Program in Religion and in conjunction with a Colloquy on Kierkegaard, Wittgenstein, and Religious Belief. Bouwsma added something to it the day of the lecture and omitted some in the reading of it. Both the addition and the omission are included here. Bouwsma wrote at least three papers in connection with this theme. The two not presented here—one titled "Undigested Remarks" and the other, "Notes on Kierkegaard"—have large parts of them woven into this one.

In Kierkegaard's *The Point of View* is the following sentence:

The contents of this little book affirm, then, what I truly am as an author, that the whole of my work as an author is related to Christianity, to "the problem of becoming a Christian" with the direct or indirect polemic against "the monstrous illusion" we call Christendom, or against the illusion that in such a land as ours all are Christians of a sort.[1]

I am interested in one phrase in the sentence, namely, "the monstrous illusion." I am not especially interested in the occasion of Kierkegaard writing this little book. He wrote it, as he said, "for orientation." I assume that if this work is related to the problem of becoming a Christian, then the monstrous illusion must be an illusion concerning just that, an illusion concerning how one becomes a Christian. This man became a Christian. There was a time when he was not a Christian. Accordingly, to understand this, one must be clear concerning what he was before and how then he became something quite different, a different man. This change in a man is conceived by Kierkegaard as a radical change. The illusion is seen in that man who has scarcely changed at all or who has changed in a superficial way and

1. Soren Kierkegaard, *The Point of View for My Work as an Author*, trans. Walter Lowrie (New York: Harper and Row, 1962), p. 5 f.

who is under the impression that whatever is now different in him is the change he may have heard about and is the change described by Kierkegaard as that of becoming a Christian. A man's having been white and having become black or having been black and having become white may for our purpose be considered superficial, significant as the changes may be in the market place. The change Kierkegaard is discussing is more than skin-deep and is invisible in the market place, a change from black to white within, from darkness within to light.

Kierkegaard set himself the task of dispelling the monstrous illusion. In order to understand all this, I have got to understand what the illusion is, how it arises, and how it is to be dispelled. After notes interminable, I still feel as though I have been writing all around these things. I could say, "Nobody knows the trouble I've seen," trying, striving—one of Kierkegaard's favorite words—to compose one neat statement of what Kierkegaard was doing. I should have to see what Kierkegaard saw as he saw that. Under the circumstances the best I can do is to go on struggling on paper with you.

What then was Kierkegaard doing? He was helping us to gain some perspective of our lives. "Look! here are possibilities. And you must choose; you cannot have a life without choosing." He was not, however, merely presenting possibilities. There is more. He was more interested in filling our hearts with something like terror. You are at stake. What is to become of you? Kierkegaard writes somewhere of stirring a man to passion, waking him up out of his lethargy, by giving him a wild horse to tame, a kicking bronco, such a horse as Plato assumed every man had to tame. Perhaps a ferocious dog would do too. The problem for him was not to help a man become clear about something so that at the end he might say, "Yes, I understand. It is interesting," but to terrorize a man with tomorrow, with his tomorrow, with uncertainty, with horrible possibility; and, I must not forget, with one other possibility. The point of this is to compel a man to examine his life, to force a man to assume responsibility, "Be ye not as dumb driven cattle. Choose!" In connection with *Either-Or* a man must of his own accord come to say of himself, "Thou art the man," and this must take the form of accusation and of desperation. No man is going to understand what it means to become a Christian who does not know the fear that passeth understanding. And does this have something to do with the illusion? Indeed. For that man for whom Kierkegaard has prepared a fright is a man made acquainted with the Scriptures. He sleeps on them. "A little sleep, a little slumber, a little folding of the hands to sleep and so cometh thy (spiritual) poverty upon thee." "A knavish speech sleeps in a foolish man." So too may the terrible Scriptures. They may also sing. How are you to wake up the man who thinks he is awake? That was something like Kierkegaard's problem.

At the outset of what Kierkegaard regarded as his calling—this is what makes him a religious writer—he was confronted with what he regarded as "a monstrous illusion," "a vain conceit." Whether there was such an "illusion," such "a conceit," may be questioned. It was in this way that he conceived his task. To Kierkegaard this was a matter of passionate concern since the illusion was one which may be expressed in this way: Men thought they understood Christianity and lived in the illusion that they were Christians. The illusion made them impervious to, let us say, Jesus Christ. They kept on repeating what Jesus Christ said and this then weary language seemed as a shield against their hearing what was said. This notion one should in 1970 be able to grasp since the illusion of intelligibility is now a familiar concept. There is something sad about Kierkegaard's having to explain what he has been doing in his book since, according to his own account, the success of his work depends upon his coming upon his readers from behind. Here then he seems to have lost patience; and standing now before his readers he tells them that he is coming upon them from behind. He must have been desperate for understanding—which shows too that the intellectual talents of those whom he wanted above all to reach were ill-adjusted to get the point. So he had to explain it, which spoils the reading, as it does the joke. He says that he does this for orientation.

So we can understand Kierkegaard to be saying, "There is a monstrous illusion, a vain deceit"—and if we are to understand Kierkegaard, we had better discover what he conceived that illusion to be.

We can, having noticed this, now also understand Kierkegaard's preoccupation with the problem of dealing with an illusion. One has to be gentle, subtle, come from behind, attack indirectly, avoid any frontal attack. All these expressions, "wounding from behind," "the indirect method," "indirect communication," are associated with this task. So are the words "If you can find exactly the place where the other is and begin there, you may, perhaps, have the luck to lead him to the place where you are" (Kierkegaard, p. 29). He, in this case, is under the illusion, but he is also living out his life somehow. A man of the world, who thinks he is a Christian—Kierkegaard is to lead this man to where he, Kierkegaard, is. And where is Kierkegaard? Kierkegaard, according to Kierkegaard, understands what this man does not understand, namely, Christianity. And Kierkegaard, accordingly, can lead this man to an awareness of what he is, that he lives as the seducer does or as the judge does, that he is no Christian.

I said that Kierkegaard, having conceived of his task as that of dispelling an illusion, reflected a great deal on how this is to be done. This illusion is, of course, not optical, in which case one could do whatever is to be done in such cases. Sometimes one can discover the cause and deal with it in this way. The optical illusions we are familiar with are easily corrected. Walk down the railroad tracks and you will see where the tracks meet. No deception is involved here. And if there was an occasion where you thought you saw a man behind that tree, you could keep an eye on that tree, and you might beat around the bushes and flush that man out. The illusion of which Kierkegaard speaks is of an altogether different sort. I have already described it as an illusion of intelligibility. No wonder Kierkegaard had to consider how such an illusion was to be dispelled. And that, as he conceived of it, the illusion was widespread, in this respect like the illusion of seeing the railroad tracks converge, made it all the more difficult to dispel. One man's illusion gives support to another's. And what would then correspond to walking down the railroad tracks or to walking towards the horizon to touch it when it meets the earth, deep blue all around at the end of my finger? So once again, the question is, What are you going to do? All these people are living out their lives under an illusion that prevents their even hearing the words of life, the same words which lie asleep in their illusion.

We can now see what he (Kierkegaard) says. You are not to say to them, "You are not Christians"; on the contrary, you are to treat them as Christians, treat them according to their professions, and they will soon discover by the contrast between what they are and their professions that they are not what they profess. This approach presupposes that these people who are to be helped recognize at least some part of what is involved in their professions and what other men may accordingly expect of them. This is, I take it, the occasion for irony and humor. Within this situation, as I have already indicated, Kierkegaard must be clear concerning Christianity and concerning just what the illusion is.

Here is a problem I should be able to help with: How is this sort of illusion to be dispelled? One must also consider how the illusion arises, or at any rate how Kierkegaard figured this out. I must review. It is not, let me begin, that these people did nothing with the language which Kierkegaard claims to have understood. So it will be necessary to lay that out. *What do the orthodox do with it and what do the Hegelians do? Here are grammatical aberrations.* Here is a task, too. We get, accordingly, a grammatical elaboration of the language when what is required is obedience and surrender. The elaboration is cheap in that one can indulge in that and enjoy at the same time one's intellectual respectability. This is the background against which we need to dispel the illusion. And I am not clear as to how much we can rely on Kierkegaard for the particular cases of grammatical aberration and of the intelligible gospel language.

Perhaps this is the way we begin. The first thing Kierkegaard must have been clear about is the role of the language of Scripture in this continuing association between God and a man, a Christian. It is in this association that the language has life. In those terms and in those alone is this language to be understood. Perhaps Saint Augustine's *Confessions* would serve in this way. And what in this case can a reader hear? Only what Saint Augustine says—and does: you can "hear" what God says only as what Saint Augustine says reflects this. This is consistent with what Kierkegaard says about the loneliness of the knights of faith. And in this case how do the Scriptures enter into the preparation of the Christian life? Is it as affirming a possibility? It is possible that God should speak to someone. In this way a man is alerted to hear. And then it happens. A man becomes a Christian when God speaks to him.

Here, at any rate, is the point. Kierkegaard must work out the consistency of the Christian, his life, and his language. How does God enter into the life of a man to challenge him and to promise?

In the contrasting cases one must represent the inconsistency of the language and the life. Here the same language which is a part of the environment is present, too, but whereas in the former case the language enters as a divine challenge, in this case the language rides along on the surface of the life without determining anything about the life. The picture of this must be presented, too. But perhaps this cannot be done. And that might be why Kierkegaard writes *Either-Or* without any religious language. It is pure aesthetic. "First I will show you the aesthetic. In this you should be able to recognize your life." It would be well if one could present that same life with the coating of religious language. But the point of doing this is that you should be aware of the difference between this life of yours and the religious. So the religious must also be exhibited. Now do you see what you are, that your life is this, aesthetic or ethical, and not religious, or if religious, not Christian? What I need, however, is the form of these lives, expressed in, or rather as, the language of those who live these lives. Expression of desire, the imperative, prayer. In each case, the life, pursuit of pleasure, obedience, and faithfulness, throughout one's days—these are the drama of one's existence.

Saint Augustine would furnish the exemplar. Here you see *in his language* what he is concerned about, what he rejoices in, what he fears, what his suffering is.

These people say, "We are Christians." How now is "I am a Christian" to be understood? I think, as a vow, as a pledge. But how are these people supposed to understand what they are saying? Well, they can remember what they have done. They remember that they were confirmed, what their priest said, that they have over the years gone to church, on special occasions said the ceremonial words, bowed their heads, etc. This is once again where Kierkegaard makes the point: this language is the language of one who has made a decision, one who has sworn to be faithful, and who continually renews his vows and rejoices in doing so. In language he vows, and in language he rejoices. He is not noting a fact. This is all a part of Kierkegaard's discussion: what it means to become a Christian. One does not become a Christian automatically, smoothly, but rather by a deep wrenching of one's nature, in which one takes part in decision and in suffering.

Kierkegaard states his problem in these terms, "What it means to be a Christian." If being a Christian is the description of a certain form of life, not from the cradle to the grave, but from a certain time in one's life to the grave—then Kierkegaard has only to distinguish being a Christian from being this or that, which may be mistaken for being a Christian. This may be better: there is being a Christian; there is also being under the illusion one is a Christian. The latter takes at least two forms. The first is described as "living in aesthetic categories"; the second, in ethical categories. In the former, one lives by pleasant drift; in the latter, by one's duty, set down as commands, requirements, etc. The task of explaining the illusion is the task of describing how the language of Christianity is assimilated to an altogether different sort of life. The language is as a bed of roses, no thorns, in which "I lay me down to sleep," "God will keep me, rocks my cradle." The gospel is like music, music to live by, rock-a-by baby, the lullaby one may hear on Sunday. The gospel describes how things are, and like the great system of Hegel, assures us that all is well. The gospel is my sleeping bag, "I shall not want." Given this assurance—tonight I will sleep—I can spend my days as I please. It is a guarantee, God's word for it, with the imprimatur of Hegel, that no matter what, I am taken care of. After all, the devil can cite Scripture for his purpose, so why should not a man who has other purposes. The 23rd psalm is beautiful. What then is missing in that psalm?

I am suggesting that the illusion that one is a Christian arises out of a misunderstanding of the language. Is it a matter of leaving out the ethical? Is it a matter of overlooking the ethical? If Christianity is not in some way present, the language must be there; otherwise the illusion would not be present. This introduces the idea of illusion again. "I am a Buddhist." Could a similar illusion arise in this case? Can a man be under the illusion that he is ethical, that he is a servant under God— when he is not? Does the ethical too involve the idea of challenge and decision? I think not. But I do not know.

*   *   *

When Kierkegaard was here, Christianity was his subject. What led him to discuss this? An illusion, or a whole nest of illusions. I'm inclined to think now it's a whole mess. So if I've repeated myself, I'm always referring to another illusion or illusions concerning what it means to become a Christian. That is the question to which, according to Kierkegaard, he devotes his thought. He is an intellectual combatant, a fighter, against an illusion. That is one reason why Kierkegaard devotes so much attention to the subject of dispelling the illusion—the task determines the method. As I see it now, the way to dispel an illusion is not by presenting the subject in a direct way—one must change the person who is under the illusion. No one is going to understand what it means to become a Christian until he has first understood what such a man is before he becomes a Christian. Those young friends of Socrates also had to come to understand something about themselves before they could join Socrates in asking his questions. All of us who learn from Wittgenstein had to come to understand something about ourselves, about our confusions, before we could return to where we were when as children we understood. Philosophy is generally an ailment which children don't have. There is no commonsense answer to a philosophical problem—hence the way is a long way round.

Those of us who believed all sorts of impossible things about an impossible father and who became angry when someone said, "You have no such father," have first to become acquainted with ourselves as unconscious wishers who give birth to our own fathers. I think you must recognize Freud in that. All such treatments are occasions of offense, even of anger and resistance. The illusion is a vested interest, and accordingly the change may require struggle, patience, and humiliation. It is not easy for those persons in Copenhagen to endure Kierkegaard—nor easy for those intellectuals young and old in Athens to thank Socrates for robbing them. It has not been easy for some of us to loose our minds of the grammatical folly which in the good days ensured our metaphysical security. Where are our feet now? And have not many men run away from their analysts fighting the battle for their wishes, dreading the world, and themselves laid bare without the cover of unconscious make-believe? I do not know. In all these cases, the sources of the illusion are not out there as it is in the sunlight on the water that produces the bent stick. The sources are in us. Is there, then, sunlight in us that bends sticks? Not exactly sunlight. Not exactly sticks.

> Father, Oh Father, what do we hear
> In this land of unbelief and fear?
> The land of dreams is better far
> Above the light of the morning star.

Let us begin with the illusion again—the what *is.* "God came into the room," Toto says, "to shake a man's hand, to sit by the side of his bed, to sup with him, to wash his feet, to give him a coat. But the man drew back, would not shake his hand, moved over on the bed, would not eat with him, nudged aside the basin of water, refused the coat. He wanted first to know who this was that came into his room. 'Who are you? What are your credentials?' But the visitor would only say, 'I came to teach you to shake another man's hand. The other man is a stranger. He is your neighbor. To sit by the side of another man's bed; to sup with him; to wash his feet; to give him a coat (yours).' Again the man drew back. He did not want to do these things. The visitor did not leave. He said, 'Receive from me and receive not only what I give but receive my giving, and you will then be transformed. For you will then have received the gift of giving, which others may then receive. In receiving my gift and my giving you will have received the gift of giving, and in doing so you will have received me.' " Suppose he then went on " 'In receiving me you will have received eternal life, for I am eternal life.' " Would that man, or any other man, have understood? If now this man congratulates himself upon having had such a visitor and remembers every word that was said and enjoys reciting what was said, cherishing even the tone of voice, and reveling in the teaching, he is under an illusion. How is one to enjoy a two-edged sword?

*   *   *

"What it means to be a Christian"—that is how Kierkegaard describes the subject of his investigation. That he should investigate this subject shows that there has been some confusion concerning this. There were those people who said, "I am a Christian" and of whom Kierkegaard then said they were under an illusion. His task, as he conceived it, was to dispel that illusion.

Here then are some expressions: "I am a Christian," "He is a Christian," etc., and the question is as to how such expressions are to be understood. Here the whole question of "understanding"—what is it to understand?—arises. What would one have to know about someone in order to know that he is a Christian or *can one not know that at all?* What must such a man who indeed is a Christian have understood and what must have happened to him? Kierkegaard makes a point of this: if a man in 1970 is a Christian, then there must have been a time before that, when he became a Christian, and in order for him to have become a Christian, that is, something which he was not before, then he must have been something different before. What was that? In terms of the distinction between the aesthetic and the ethical, should we say that a man can become a Christian only after he has become ethical? I guess we are to say this, too: A man becomes ethical. In that case, too, he must have become something and been something different before. So there is this spiritual progress from the aesthetic through the ethical to the religious. First, years of the aesthetic—for most of my life I was a boy. Then I became serious and found a master whom I tried to serve. ("The law is the schoolmaster which brought me into Christ.") It bore down upon me like a burden, a heavy load. And then came one who lifted the burden. If this is right, then the task, what it means to be a Christian, involved no narrow investigation but is one of the possibilities of human life.

These are what sort of problems? Problems of language. What is a man to do in life? Here are possibilities:

Enjoy, Enjoy,
Serve God,
Love God, Believe, Hope.

What I wanted to use was the idea of the variety of language games. Consider how one might be under the illusion he was a Christian because each year he traveled to Oberammergau and viewed the Passion

Play. He felt so sorry for the Lord Jesus. So there is a gospel story. It may be dramatized, played, and a motion picture may be made of it. And we can imagine that it is well done. It is an affecting story. We might compare it to a Greek play or to a similar stage production based on the little we know of Socrates. Then we could discuss it. Is it a tragedy? What would Aristotle say? That this was a play about Jesus Christ and Jesus Christ is the central figure of Christianity and we might admit to some bias in favor of the play for his sake, might make us all feel like Christians. How moving, how beautiful it is, this play about Jesus Christ! In this case, it must be pointed out, one can see and enjoy the play, and after the theater, one can go on as usual, and on occasion one can quote lines from the play; there are quotable, memorable lines.

Can the problem be put in this way: In 1970, as in 1820, men had between themselves and nothing only the Scriptures? Among most people in 1970 the Scriptures mean nothing. Most men have heard of the Scriptures. The Bible is still among the best selling books. In this way it ranks with *Portnoy's Complaint* and *Uncle Tom's Cabin*. So the book is much seen but not much read. There are, however, many people who read it and there are still many people who hear it read and explained, in bits, that is. Here now is my question: Everyone of those who reads it may say that he understands it. At least there are many who read it and say they understand it. To every man his own understanding of it. Is someone now in a position to say, someone among those who read it and say they understand it, in a position to say that he understands it and that those others are under the illusion that they understand it? In any case Kierkegaard is one of those who says this, "I understand it and those others do not understand it." Whether Kierkegaard does understand may for the present be set aside. *What is interesting to me at present is how he understands these illusions and how he goes on to try to dispel the illusions.* For we are, as Kierkegaard was, returned again to something like the principles of the human understanding. What is it to understand? Shall we say that as there are varieties of language games so too there are varieties of understanding? I think that will be a good idea.

I know how one might go about this were this a straight philosophical confusion. There would be language we all understand to which we could appeal and there would be other language which is confused, as is shown by the grammatical hubbub. And in the present case we should have this language and that other language. We could say one is not the other. I guess it isn't like that. At least one can see how the misunderstanding of the Scriptures in the case of the aesthetic is nothing confused. Here the difference can be put in this way: Who says them? And now the understanding of what is said is determined by this. Do you understand that it is God who speaks?

The question is as to how much of what Kierkegaard describes as the illusion is to be described as grammatical. I noticed above that how one understands in the case of the Scriptures depends on who it is one understands is speaking. But it is not that one investigates and so discovers who it is that is speaking. *How one understands is shown by the way in which one reacts.* Here, two things must be clear. One must be clear concerning just what is said. And now there are these differences in responses. In the case of the aesthetic *who says*, whatever it is, it is a matter of indifference. Even though it is said that this is God's word, God might as well be the man next door. The reader enjoys what he reads and might like to know who the author is. Such a reader then may make the sort of remarks a literate literary man would make. "Socrates died like a hero; Jesus Christ like a God." There is in this case no illusion. *The illusion comes in only as one confuses this reading with that of a Christian reading.* "I remember how religious I used to feel on Christmas day, thinking of the story of Jesus's birth and hearing the music and the words of Christmas. Every year I used to look forward to the thrill of Christmas Eve." One appreciates the gospel as a story, "the old, old story": this story is one of the oldest and most beautiful. It is the beautiful story. A man who got his students to appreciate the story and the exquisite language of the Scriptures might well think that he was doing God service. And he was. Apollo's. And why should not the Seducer of the Diary have had the good taste to read portions, the loveliest of the Scriptures, to provide a modicum of the odor of sanctity to her undoing? For there is the odor of sanctity.

Reading the Scriptures in this way is one thing. Reading them in this way under the illusion that this is Christian, is another.

It seems to me now that I have described the aesthetic reading, whereas Kierkegaard describes the aesthetic life—a life lived in aesthetic categories. Insofar as those of us who live our lives in aesthetic categories, read in the way in which we live, how we read will make little difference. Whether we read them for "the beauty of it,' or whether we read them for the purported knowledge they give us, in either case they leave our lives untouched. Decision—a primary concept in Kierkegaard—is not involved. This is, however, the reading of the Scriptures which bears the brunt of his criticism and scorn. The Scriptures are regarded as a form of revealed metaphysics, especially described for

God's children, those who lisp; and not for God's mature co-workers, to whom God can speak as his equals. God in this case depends on their mature intelligence to interpret and to amplify by proofs and other helps for the elite who no longer lisp or never did lisp. Those who know a great deal already, the learned, know how to avail themselves of what knowledge is provided in the Scriptures and how to incorporate that into the whole body of knowledge which they also can provide.

> The Scriptures as an aesthetic feast. (A feast of lights.)
> The Scriptures as knowledge.
> The Scriptures as ethics.
> The Scriptures as challenge and promise.

If we regard Wittgenstein as teaching us how to read, and, of course, not only how to read, but to speak as well, reading and discussing philosophy, we may in the same way, or in a similar way, regard Kierkegaard as teaching us how to read and to discuss the Scriptures. There are in both cases illusions of intellegibility which have given rise to the need in each case. The illusions which have produced the expressions of confusion we describe as philosophy come about through misconceptions concerning the workings of our language, misconceptions which may operate either consciously or unconsciously. Those misconceptions, misgrammars, the main ones, have been identified by Wittgenstein for our guidance. If one is aware that there are these common misconceptions, one may be on the alert to detect them as the source of one's own trouble. If you bump your head against an invisible wall, you may want to know what that wall is and how to avoid it. Among these is the idea that language is always read in the same way, namely, to communicate thoughts; we are always communicating thoughts. Now in connection with Christianity there is a similar illusion. Men have treated the Scriptures as God's way of giving us certain information which God no doubt did his best to communicate but which he obviously had to do as though he were talking to children, which he was. To others he communicated in clearer, and one might say, scientific, *wissenschaft,* language. Here there is an illusion. And how does it arise? Through a misconception of the role of language, and, I guess, of God. Here we meet the same idea, "Language is used in only one way." This is a prejudice, a recent one. The idea, however, is also present in Kierkegaard, that God who is almost highest would be concerned only about what is highest and what is highest is that man should know. So the original prejudice is fortified by the idea that knowledge is best.

In this way the illusion of intelligibility of the Scriptures—a certain reading of the Scriptures—is explained. The Scriptures are not a body of knowledge, a hyper-metaphysical revelation, to be culled and arranged for the intellectual who, once the essence of the Scriptures has been distilled, may now go on to higher things.

So there is an analogy in what we may describe as the logical aspects of these investigations. There is illusion in both cases. The task in both cases is conceived of as that of dispelling illusions. The illusion is in both cases one of misunderstanding certain languages. Here I see that I must be careful. Both those who seek to understand ordinary language, and those who seek to understand the Scriptures run into confusion due to mistaken expectations concerning what the language must mean. Let me get this straight. In the work of Wittgenstein there is ordinary language we understand. That ordinary language is related to words or expressions that give us trouble. In ordinary language we discover the corrective of the language which expresses the confusion. In the work of Kierkegaard there corresponds to ordinary language in Wittgenstein the language of Scriptures, which Kierkegaard understands. Without this latter assumption Kierkegaard cannot be effective. And this is not how it is in Wittgenstein. There, ordinary language is taken to be language which we all understand. Here, there is agreement. But Kierkegaard's task is in that way more formidable. He has first to teach us how to understand the language of Scripture. Or should I say that he has only to remind us of how he does, and has all along, understood it: *the key to the understanding of the Scriptures is the promise of eternal life.* At least we should be able to come to an understanding of what Kierkegaard is · about. The differences and similarities between Wittgenstein and Kierkegaard should help to sharpen our understanding.

"What is Christianity?" is the wrong question. It evokes such answers as that it is a view, which leads to the idea that a Christian is someone who holds that view. He stands on a hill, "a God kissing hill" and looks. A Christian is someone who looks. He very likely enjoys the view. Here is another answer: Christianity is a philosophy, a philosophy of life. A philosopher is someone who has some beliefs, and so, too, a Christian is someone who has certain beliefs. But what now makes this man, this Christian, a philosopher? It is just that he has those beliefs. If he is a full-fledged philosopher, he will go on to show you how reasonable those beliefs are. He may tell you that what he believes is true and may prove to you that it is true. He is an intellectual. And if he does not have the proof, he believes that God does. Kierkegaard does not ask this question and in this way avoids such answers. Instead he asks, "What does it mean to be a Christian?" and the corollary to that, "What does it mean to become a Christian?" This is one of the strokes of his genius, for it introduces a new and fresh perspective for understanding the church steeple. The latter question, particularly, stresses the dramatic character of the Christian life. For to be a Christian now is earlier to have met someone and ever since then to have lived in his company. To become a Christian involves having met someone. People's lives are often changed in that way. "I met someone."

Miss Anscombe on Faith

Bouwsma presented this paper in response to a paper of Elizabeth Anscombe's entitled "Faith." Both were read at the "Annual Oregon Colloquium in Philosophy" at the University of Oregon in April 1968.

The subject is faith and the question is, What is faith? I want to call attention to the peculiar nature of the question. We are all acquainted with such peculiar questions as, What is thinking? What is believing? Compared to these questions our present question is peculiarly peculiar. I'll explain that. In response to the question, What is thinking? Wittgenstein could write, "Can one think without speaking?—And what is thinking? Well, don't you ever think? Can't you observe yourself and see what is going on? It should be quite simple. You do not have to wait for it as for an astronomical event, and then perhaps make your observation in a hurry."[1] Much the same sort of response might be made to the question What is believing? But no such response is possible to the question What is faith? Here we cannot say, "Well, you have faith, don't you? Can't you observe yourself?" We might be more inclined to say that indeed it is more like an astronomical event. But then, since it is also a miracle, we should add that it cannot be observed even in a hurry. Suppose we say, "Find someone who has faith and ask him." But how are we to find him? If a man says that

1. Ludwig Wittgenstein, *Philosophical Investigations*, trans. G. E. M. Anscombe (New York: Macmillan, 1953), s. 327, p. 106e.

he has faith, are we to trust him? May he not have something quite different from faith? The philosophical questions alluded to above arise out of language we are all familiar with and understand. That also assures us of our being able to answer these questions or at least of our coming to see that we agree concerning what it is we agree about. We could not get on if we did not in common understand the language. Here we have reminders we can work with. But the word "faith" is more like a word in a foreign language and even as some would say in a dead language. If God is dead, the word "God" is dead. And so too the word "faith." In what sense foreign? Our situation might be compared to this: We overhear a man we see or can see in communication with someone or something we can neither hear nor see. We cannot understand what the man is saying in this communication because what is said is intelligible only if one can also hear what is said to him by the someone on the other side of the wall. We can hear the man speak and we can then after this strange happening observe that he does certain surprising and perilous things. His doing these things may seem to us to have something to do with that conversation. This is partly wrong. He tells us that it has something to do with it. We may say that this man has had a conversation with The Unknown. The Unknown told him to do these things. I am going to parody this language again: So we could imagine a human being who spoke only in what seemed to be a monologue and who always did this kneeling and with his eyes closed. An explorer who watched him and listened to what he said might recognize the words as familiar, might try to connect what the man was saying with what the man was doing. But he still would not be able to understand the man. And the man himself could only say that he was told by some Unknown whom he called "God" to do these things and who also promised extraordinary things, things without parallel.

I was saying that the question What is faith? is peculiarly peculiar, and *that* because the word "faith" is like a word in a foreign language. Will it do to say that the word is a word current in certain communities or communions and these people seem to understand one another? It is part of the condition of entering the community, a community of language, that one submits to learning the language to which the word "faith" belongs. There may be some question as to how many learn it or whether any do. For it is one thing to teach and another to learn, and it is in this case sometimes complained that the teachers themselves have not learned. Who, for instance, can pray? It is also said that the Unknown is the teacher, for it is a language which is spoken, read, and sung only when he is present, and how should one know what to say unless the Unknown gave the instructions. Those outside the community can hear what these people say and can overhear too what the instructions are so they can see something of how these people came to learn—if they learn. One could also imitate these people. But imitating them would not go beyond doing what these people do out here in the open. Faith is not anything one can imitate. One cannot imitate being the receiver of such a gift as faith.

II

Why believe?

Our only chance.

Is this the problem: How is one who believes, having made a confession of his beliefs, to explain this to another?

What might be understood about faith by anyone? I wish Miss Anscombe had answered that first. Miss Anscombe asks, What can be understood about faith by someone who does not have any? At least she wants to say what can be understood by such a one. The answer, as far as I can make out, is "not much," though presumably anyone can come to understand as much about faith as Russell did and as Bierce did.[2] In her discussion she says, "So an atheist can comfortably speak of faith as believing God, *can accept that formula*, if only he can ascribe a sense to belief that God speaks." But he cannot do this. She continues, "And it is because God cannot be so identified that we don't know what it is to believe that God speaks." (She has explained the "so identified.") This language troubles me. The discussion began with, "What can be understood about faith by someone who did not have any," and ends with "We don't know," which here is, I take it, the same as, "We don't understand what it is to believe that God speaks." So it seems that in the end the believer and the unbeliever are in respect to this in the same state. They cannot understand, they do not know. God is the Unknown.

This may be the right place to interpose with the question "What can be understood about faith by someone who has faith?" or "What must be understood about faith by someone who has faith?" Is the difference between the believer and the unbeliever that he can identify God as the one and only true God and therefore can also know what it is to believe that God speaks?

Miss Anscombe's comment on Russell's definition of faith as "certainty without proof" is "This seems correct." Why "seems"? Her com-

2. Ambrose Bierce, *The Devil's Dictionary* (New York: Dover, 1958).

ment on Bierce's definition[3] is, "Then it follows that Bierce's definition holds too." These, the definitions, I guess, are examples of what can be said about faith. Miss Anscombe can also say these things about faith. Presumably she can say more than they can, though I am not clear about this. What, for the moment, strikes me is that if she says that what Russell says seems correct and that what Bierce says holds, too, then she and Russell and Bierce must be looking at the same thing. They are certainly not all staring at the sentence "Faith is believing God." I am not saying that they are all looking at the same thing. I am only saying that if we are to say that Miss Anscombe is right in saying that what Russell says is, or seems correct, and Bierce's definition holds, then there are a number of us who are looking at the same thing. We cannot, of course, be looking at faith, for as with God no man hath seen faith. Having written this down, I am reminded of what our Lord said of the centurion: "I say unto you, I have not found so great faith, no not in all Israel." So faith may be found. I do not suppose that Miss Anscombe was, with the others, looking at the example of the centurion. And I must admit that I was not doing so either. I must add that I am excluding the possibility that Russell and Bierce did not know, could not have told us, what they were talking *about*. We might admit this, admit further that in a way what they said was correct (superficial grammar) and yet go on to say that they nevertheless did not understand what they were saying.

What I am about to say now is elementary. Russell and Bierce wrote what they wrote and what they wrote is said to be about faith. Miss Anscombe wrote about what *they* wrote. But a long time ago there were writers who wrote such things as these: "Being therefore justified by faith, we have peace with God through our Lord Jesus Christ, through whom also we have had our access by faith into this grace in which we stand; and we rejoice in hope of the glory of God. And not only so but we also rejoice in our tribulations; knowing that tribulation worketh steadfastness, and steadfastness character, and character hope, and hope putteth not to shame, because the love of God hath been shed abroad in our hearts through the Holy Spirit which was given unto us" (Rom. 5:1–5). Also: "And Abraham believed God, and it was reckoned unto him for righteousness," the same being repeated in the words "To Abraham his faith was reckoned for righteousness." "The strong shall live by faith";

3. "To believe without evidence those who tell without knowledge things without parallel." Bierce, "Faith," *The Devil's Dictionary*, p. 40.

"it is the gift of God"; "I have finished the course, I have kept the faith" (Tim. 4:7). I am well aware that I am reminding us of language which was once familiar and which even now some recognize. This language was given us, that we might be instructed, and being instructed, might come to faith. You may have recognized Miss Anscombe's sentence "Faith is believing God"—in what I quoted. And now I want to suggest that when Russell and Bierce and Miss Anscombe came to some agreement concerning what they were looking at—without that agreement discussion cannot come to an end—they all looked at that sentence about Abraham. "Abraham believed God and it was accounted unto him for righteousness." But since this sentence can be understood only as a sentence about Abraham and since the explanation of that sentence requires that we review the story, that is what we need. For, that same sentence we can read in that story—quite a surprise to find it so early. In any case it seems reasonable to assume, and a compliment, too, since it brings them together at just the right point, where the Scriptures, and Saint Paul, and the writer of the letter to the Hebrews, and so on would have them, to assume that they might be talking about Abraham. This is no more than to say that to discuss faith is to discuss the hero of faith, the exemplar of faith. For that is what he is in the Scriptures. Here certainly is a preestablished arrangement, providence, that early there should have been Abraham so that 2,000 years later Saint Paul should have had the hero of faith to lead the whole world to faith—if only it were to follow.

Now then I should like to translate Miss Anscombe's sentence in order that, slow as I am and, in a way, simple, I might come to understand better what she is doing. I confess I have to make it easy for myself and so I miss a lot. Now then this is my translation: I want to say what someone who was quite unlike Abraham, in what must be regarded as an essential respect, since he had no faith, might nevertheless understand in reading the story of Abraham. If we keep in mind that the story was given for our instruction in order that we too might become like Abraham, that may help.

Let us now imagine Russell reading the story of Abraham. There is a genealogy: "And Terah begat Abram, Nahor, and Heran." The story begins with Chapter 12. "Now Jehovah said unto Abram" and at the outset there is a command, "Get thee out of thy country," and a promise, "I will make of thee a great nation. . . ." The story of Abraham continues over the extent of twelve chapters. God speaks to Abram, and later Abraham on a number of occasions, and there are commands, and

92

the promise once made is repeated and made more definite: "And, lo, Sarah, thy wife, shall have a son." And now to the point. After Isaac has grown to a youth, the same Jehovah that promised to make of him a great nation said to him, "Take now thy son, thine only son, whom thou lovest . . . and offer him there as a burnt-offering. . . ." This then Abraham set out to do. This is the text of faith. The point then is that Abraham still believed God, that is, believed the promise. It is this that makes him the hero of faith. He believed the impossible, trusting God.

We are now prepared to see how what Russell says applies. We may understand Russell as saying, Abraham was certain without proof. Saint Paul writes, "Yet, looking unto the promise of God, he wavered not through unbelief but waxed strong through faith, giving glory to God, and being fully assured that what he had promised he was able to perform" (Rom. 4:20). Here then Abraham is described as not wavering, fully assured, believing. And as for proof there was none. There is an ambiguity here. Abraham was certain that the promise would be kept. If Russell then is saying that Abraham was certain that the promise would be kept, but he had no proof that it would, that involves a confusion. For Abraham's assurance is based on trust in God. This must then be the certainty that Russell had in mind. So Abraham believed that it was God who made the promise, and it is that certainty which was without proof. This comes to: When at the beginning Jehovah said to Abraham "Get thee out of thy country . . ." and he, Abraham, went, there is in the Scriptures no word saying that Abraham checked to find out who this was speaking and by what authority he spoke. There are, however, certain passages which may be related to this and to the issue which Suárez[4] presents. In Chapter 17 is this passage: "Jehovah appeared to Abram and said unto him, 'I am God Almighty.'" Then follows: "Walk before me and be thou perfect." If one were intent on finding an explanation of Suárez's "God reveals that he reveals," this might do. There are other announcements of that sort: "I am the God of thy fathers, . . ." (Moses, Ex. 3:6); "I am Jehovah, thy God, who brought thee out of the land of Egypt . . ." (Ex. 20). I must get back to the subject. There is no proof. But since there is no proof in the Scriptures, this shows us at the same time what does and does not make sense here.

I think I'll not go on to examine Bierce's definition. I want to return to the question as to what Russell might have understood. Is it striking

4. Francisco Suárez, Spanish Jesuit, 1548–1617. Miss Anscombe makes reference to his having created a puzzling regress about the foundation of faith in revelation.

that Russell should have been interested only in: Abraham was certain but he had no proof, and took no notice of this, that there was a command and a promise? I'll begin over again. To say that faith is believing God may be regarded as a way of drawing attention to something in the story of Abraham. Let us say then that this sentence was put there for our instruction, not to call our attention to "No proof," but in order to open up a prospect, a new possibility for us, a promise to lift us, too, higher than what may otherwise be the humdrum present and a short future on a dreary plain, more people like ourselves, overpopulation, and so on. If Russell's "No proof," which "seems correct," shuts the door on a promise, should we then say that he understood? Let me try once more. Is there anything which we should regard as understanding the story of Abraham other than one's appropriating it to one's own need? What Abraham heard is here for every man to hear. The story of Abraham is here to alert us to the possibility that there is a command-promise for everyone that hath ears to hear. The story of Abraham may be read as a dead story. In reflecting upon it one might take notice of the fact that it is about a man who is certain, and he doesn't bother about proof. That is all. It doesn't touch one otherwise. Abraham is not the sort one would want to have much to do with. How different Saint Paul or Kierkegaard! What is that story doing here? It is to help to kindle us with hope and the promise of a new day, a new human being, a new forever.

III

Do you understand that? comes to: Can you take that in? Can you digest that? If I were now asked, Do you understand Miss Anscombe's paper? I should say that I do not. I should not be able to say for whom she was writing this paper nor why she wrote it. Perhaps if I stayed with it for some years I could do better. I might get to understand it. I can understand for whom Kierkegaard wrote and why he wrote. He wrote for those who as he said were under an illusion that they understood Christianity. Hence he had to remove the illusion. These people read the Scriptures, as they supposed, to find out something, to become acquainted with its teachings, and to exercise in this a hyperfastidiousness, making something precise, just right. There is an intellectualism of the word just as there is a preciousness in the law. Men spend their lives dotting *i*'s and crossing *t*'s, getting every "but" and "if" and "therefore" well fashioned, just as there were men counting the seeds of mint and anise and cummin in order to make sure that these tithes were tithes and not one seed under the tithe or over. Once the *t*'s were crossed and the *i*'s dotted men could live secure. The answers in the catechism assured one of eternal life. The language of the Scriptures, misunderstood in this way, killed and stuffed in human heads, presented Kierkegaard with the problem of taking this language out into the open and breathing life into it again. This now I understand. But in the sense in which I understand Kierkegaard I do not understand Miss Anscombe. She does not, for instance, begin with some misunderstanding, unless one were to say that there is some misunderstanding concerning what unbelievers understand about faith. But she does not tell us what that is. If the misunderstanding about faith is the counterpart of the misunderstanding that Kierkegaard is also concerned about, then it must be that faith is either a matter of knowledge or it is judged so—as being irrelevant or inadequate because it is not knowledge, groundless opinion, or hearsay. Perhaps this is it: she is telling us that the reason why Russell and Bierce cannot understand faith is that they cannot understand the gospel and they cannot understand that because they are expecting something which can be or is subject, if not to proof, to the attempt to prove. They are prompted to ask, How do you know? and this frame of mind is a barrier. There is no such "how" about it. This expectation is shown in the use of the expressions "without proof" and "without evidence" and "without knowledge." In matters without parallel, the greater is the requirement that there be evidence or proof, for here one cannot rely on probability as we can in matters with parallel. "His eye is on the sparrow." Is he then a bird-watcher? That would have a parallel.

What persuades me above all that I do not understand her is the last paragraph of her paper. "What we can say is this: The supposition that an adult has faith—believes something by faith—is the supposition that he has the thought: 'This (what he has been hearing from a teacher, perhaps) is from God, and therefore I believe it'; *and* that what he so believes is true; and that he has no other evidence of it; perhaps, for it to be a matter of faith in the strictest sense, that he could have no other evidence of it." It may be that Miss Anscombe can say this. I cannot say it. I cannot imagine myself supposing this nor of what adult I should suppose it, what about him would lead me to do this, or what I should do this for. If all that Miss Anscombe means to say is that this is how she imagines it, well, that is how she imagines it. She might also have in mind that this is, as a matter of fact, how some people she knows who came to faith have actually reported how it was with them. If that is the case, such reports might be of some interest. We can imagine such a person, then, having told about having been in Oxford on a certain day when she heard this man saying or when she saw this man sitting on a bench reading his Bible and she asked him what he was reading and the man pointed out a verse in the book of Romans . . . and then "I had the thought . . . , etc." Having a thought for the purported occasion seems tame indeed, nothing like the desperate cry of Pilgrim when he cried, "What must I do?" There is no fear and trembling. God comes along like these thoughts marching in single file. When, I should like to ask, were we instructed concerning what such a man would be like? This takes us back again to Abraham. Once more, then, in the exemplary case nothing is said about his having said that he had such and such thoughts, nor is it said by another that he had such thoughts, such thoughts as any alert epistemologist might be expected to have. May we then conclude that Miss Anscombe weaves a surroundings for the expression "Jehovah said," surroundings which reflect her present interest, but such surroundings as we do not find in the story of Abraham or Moses or Saint Paul. Not many people would say that Miss Anscombe has improved on the story of Abraham—should we say for our edification?

I should like to add this: It is certainly a mistake to think of faith as what happened on a certain occasion, such as a man's having had this and that thought. It is the whole story of Abraham in terms of which we must understand him as the exemplar of faith. And it is the story not as seen from the outside, as by Sarah, who laughed, and presumably Abraham is the only one who did not laugh, but as seen from the inside, in that silence in which Abraham heard God speak.

There are, however, two examples, one from Saint Augustine, hence as nearly authentic as we can get, and another from Dostoevsky in the story of the Mysterious Visitor, hence fictional, which might be helpful in some way. Saint Augustine shows us how he remembered what, on that occasion, happened. And Dostoevsky, in this story, shows us how he imagined a happening of a similar sort.

I want to try out how Miss Anscombe's supposition provides a form for the supposition that Saint Augustine has the thought "This voice as of a boy or girl, I know not which, coming from a neighboring house, chanting, and oft-repeating, 'Take up and read; Take up and read' is from God." Saint Augustine provides, as we might expect, more detail. He writes, "Immediately my countenance was changed and I began most earnestly to consider whether it was usual for children in any kind of game to sing such words; nor could I remember ever to have heard the like. So, restraining the torrent of my tears, I rose up, interpreting it in no other way than as a command to me from heaven to open the book and to read the first chapter I should light upon." Saint Augustine has an explanation for that too. "For I had heard of Antony, that, accidentally coming in while the gospel was being read, he received the admonition as if what was read was addressed to him, 'Go and sell that thou hast and give to the poor, and thou shalt have treasure in heaven; come and follow me.' And by such an oracle was he forthwith converted unto thee." Here is another case of hearing God. We may accordingly suppose that Antony heard this, the gospel being read, and then what? That he had the thought "This is from God and therefore . . . and so it is true; and there is no evidence for it. . . ." It's a good thing that Antony studied philosophy in Cambridge or he could never have had such thoughts and so could never have had faith. This must be the case too with that centurion mentioned earlier. As for Saint Augustine, he writes, "restraining the torrent of my tears"—something Miss Anscombe does not mention—"I rose up, interpreting it in no other way than as a command to me from heaven." Should we understand this as Augustine's having such and such a sequence of pretty dry thoughts?

Here is the passage from Dostoevsky. I should mention that in Saint Augustine's *Confessions* and in the story of the Mysterious Visitor there is what goes before and leads up to the incidents here related. The Mysterious Visitor is a man who some years earlier committed a murder. He has come to talk to Father Zossima. I'll break into the conversation:

"Go and confess," is whispered to him. My voice failed me, but I whispered it firmly. Then I took up the New Testament from the table, the Russian Translation, and showed him the gospel of St. John, ch. 12, verse 24: "Verily, verily, I say unto you, Except a corn of wheat fall into the ground and die, it abideth alone; but if it die, it bringeth forth much fruit."

I had read that verse before he came in. He read it.

"That's true," he said, but he smiled bitterly. "Yes," he said after a short pause, "it's awful the things you come across in those books. It's easy to push them under your nose. And who wrote them? Not men, surely."

"The Holy Spirit wrote them," I said.

"It's easy for you to talk," he said, smiling again, but almost with hatred this time.

I took the book again, opened it in another place and showed him the epistle to the Hebrews, ch. 10, verse 31. He read, "It is a fearful thing to fall into the hands of the living God."

He read it and flung down the book. He was shaking all over.

"A dreadful verse," he said, "you picked out a good one, I must say." He got up from the chair. "Well," he said, "Fare well. Perhaps I shan't come again. . . . We shall meet in heaven. So it's fourteen years since I've 'fallen into the hands of God.' That is what we must call the fourteen years, mustn't we? Tomorrow I shall entreat those hands to let me go."[5]

These passages from Saint Augustine and from Dostoevsky occurred to me, not first of all as useful in helping us to understand faith but as examples of what Miss Anscombe might be thinking of when she speaks of God's speaking. In the example of Saint Augustine the first word comes in the guise of children's voices as from nowhere. And the voice sings a command. This voice—how strange—"interpreted as a command to him from heaven," leads him on to "open the book and to read," and here he reads what precisely fits his present state. (The shoe fits and he puts it on.) He is to make a radical break with his present manner of life. Am I wrong now in insisting upon our taking notice of these two details, namely, "immediately my countenance changed"— terror, perhaps,—God does not pat your wrist—and "so restraining the torrent of my tears"?—the storm in which the radical break takes place, repentance, scalding tears. So we have the command. And there must be a promise. As for the Mysterious Visitor there are no children's voices to give the alarm. Father Zossima has prepared for his coming and shows him a verse of Scripture. His response is, "It's awful the things you come across in those books." Again, terror, and in that terror the submission to an authority over him, but not complete. "He smiled bitterly." And then, "Who wrote them?" Again, "It's easy for you to talk"—which shows that he has understood what he read as a command. Father Zossima shows him another verse: " 'It is a fearful thing to fall into the hands of the living God.' He flung down the book. He was shaking all over. 'A dreadful verse,' he said." Both these passages may remind us that coming to faith is not a tranquil matter of believing God. And neither is keeping the faith. There is terror and tears, and fear and trembling, a requirement with power. And there is promise. "Tomorrow I shall entreat those hands to let me go." The discussion of faith without bringing into the light the surroundings of tortured souls, souls tried, tormented between a requirement too great and a confidence and strength too feeble—"Walk before me and be thou perfect"—is barren. Abraham was not an epistemologist. Imagine: "Without proof I can do nothing." The Scripture says, "Without me ye can do nothing."

5. Fyodor Dostoevsky, *The Brothers Karamazov*, trans. Constance Garnett (New York: Norton, 1976), p. 288f.

Adventure in Verification

Bouwsma read this paper at the Wheaton Conference on Christian Philosophy in 1963.

Get into perspective, how it is with us. And let us use for this purpose a variation on the phantasy of Kafka. We live in a city and it's up-to-date. So, of course, there are telephones. People in the city talk to each other over the telephone. They order groceries, gossip, spread the news, find out what time it is, call the police, and so on. But there are a number of people in the city who use the telephone for a quite different purpose. And to some of the other people in the town this is a great mystery. They sometimes ask, "Who are you calling?" and the reply is "We are calling the president or the king." "And what do you say to him?" "We thank him for daily bread. We thank him for all sorts of things, sunshine, for instance. And we ask for help and ask him, too, to bear with us, and so on. We carry on a regular conversation." "And does he speak to you too?" "Of course. He gives us orders, makes us promises, exhorts us, encourages us when we falter. He is kind. Sometimes he calls. That can be frightening, too." It happens now and then that one of these people will ask, "And could I listen in?" but then when he does, he hears nothing, not even a busy buzz. It sounds to him more like a disconnected phone. After that he is at first still more puzzled. It even occurs to him that the trouble lies in his ears. He soon gets over that. He goes on asking questions. Has so-

and-so ever seen the President? The answer to that is that, of course, he hasn't, that no man has ever seen the President, none of these people who make calls has seen the President. The fact is that the President is invisible. The man shakes his head. "An invisible President!" "And how then did you ever get involved in this? speaking over the telephone and having regular conversations with an invisible President?" To this the reply is not so ready. "How did he get involved in this?" He finally manages to say that at home such calls were a regular part of their daily life, as daily as bread. In emergencies there were special calls. But hadn't it ever occurred to him that the whole thing might be a hoax? An invisible President! No, it never had, though of course he had heard such talk. He had never paid any attention to it and it had never affected his devotion to the telephone.

Now consider this situation. There are people living in the city. There are mountains nearby and one especially high mountain. When these people are about to make an expedition, sailing ships to Yort over the wine-dark sea, they sacrifice an ox to Zeus, and they implore Zeus to keep the wind in their sails and to direct their darts and arrows to their targets. There are others in the company of Zeus, such as Athena and Apollo. These gods have their favorites and they play out their rivalries by playing their favorites against one another, particularly on the battlefield. Sometimes Athena sends a cloud to enshroud Achilles in order that when he is in peril Hector may not be able to find him. There are other occasions when the people take alarm and look toward that high mountain. This happens when disaster strikes, as for instance when a dragon roars outside the city or when pestilence or flood or famine overwhelms the populace. "What have we done?" they exclaim. For disaster is a sure sign of guilt. The priest may assure them that it is Zeus that is angry, for there is an unclean thing in the city, no doubt, a man afflicted with hubris. They seek him out, send him into exile, and the curse is lifted. And then at a public ceremony they sacrifice another ox. This is the symbol of reconciliation.

Now imagine a stranger who has come to the city, a brother of Xenophanes, and a great-grandfather of Euripides. He hears all this talk about Zeus and Athena and the quarrels and the curses and the roasting of the ox and naturally he doesn't understand it. "Zeus?" he asks. "In Melos and in Athens we too have suffered disasters, but we know nothing of Zeus." And then in awed tones they tell the brother of Xenophanes about Zeus and the whole company of the gods who take so much interest in what human beings do and in their expeditions. He listens but says nothing. When they have finished he asks, "And did you say that they live on Mount Olympus and drink nectar and eat ambrosia and that their blood is ichor?" He is obviously fascinated. Still it seems that he does not believe a word of it. He is determined however to find out for himself. "And," he asked, "have you ever been on Mount Olympus?" They exclaim at this. "Of course not. No man in his senses would approach Mount Olympus. Such a man could not live." They are horrified. A human being peeping through the shrubbery and prowling the heights of Olympus! He is, however, not in the least discomfited by this. He has already determined, like Prometheus, to make the ascent, expecting to find nothing on the heights of Mount Olympus but a cover of scrub oak and a scattering of mountain goats nibbling on the high ridges.

And now what do you think happened?

He climbed the mountain one moonlit night. Actually it was, as mountain climbing goes, not difficult. It was nothing compared to Everest or even Rainier. He made it easily. When he got to the top however he was surprised. The whole of the mountain top was fringed with an impenetrable jungle-growth of shrubs, trees, and vines. He could neither climb over nor get through. It made him apprehensive. "Surely," he said to himself, "this was planted to keep prowlers out." And he began, for the first time, finding himself near believing, to wonder which of the gods was the gardener. It surprised him. There was, however, nothing to do now but go back down into the city to get his hatchet. He was, however, considerably sobered by that wall of greenery and he made this second ascent with fear. It would be a frightening thing if he were to come upon strong and fierce men on the other side of the wall whose secret place he was breaking into. And what if there were giants there? He did not expect even now to find Zeus and the company of immortals. He went about cutting his way through the brambles and vines with a fast-beating heart. What if . . . ? What if . . . ?

At last, working through seven days and seven nights he cut his way through the wall. Even then there was just enough room for him to struggle through and the branches closed round the opening. He saw no one, no man, no giant, no god. At least he thought he did not. And he thought he too was seen by no man, no giant, no god. This gave him courage. Before him stood a palace of white marble, not as large as the Pentagon, but still a large and sumptuous edifice, in a style now known as Olympian. If, as he supposed, there were no Zeus and no Apollo, etc., here, at least the architecture was a worthwhile surprise. He broke through the brush about dawn, looked about him, and decided that the better part of valor and verification would be to wait and then to explore under cover of darkness. So he returned again into the wall. It would be too bad after all his work to be sent tumbling down the mountain by an angry guard perhaps twice his own size. He forgot to bring his Greek opera glasses. So he waited. Someone has said that a good part of verification is waiting.

Darkness seemed to be late that night. But it finally came. He could make out lights coming on down in the city below. Here and there a candle burned, the candle of some sculptor working overtime, and in an open plain to the right a man was running with a torch upraised, no doubt practicing for a race. Torch races were very common in those days. He saw a few lights on boats and reflected in the water, a pretty sight, and a new thing in the Piraeus, just having come in with a new ordinance recently instituted by the Eleven or the Thirty-Two or somebody else. The moon had waned by this time, so that when darkness came it was very dark. It was no fun crouching there among the brambles. He was scratched too. But suddenly the whole mountain top was ablaze with light and the whole palace glowed. He was amazed and enchanted. It was beautiful! For a moment he was overwhelmed with the splendor and he forgot why he had come. Fountains played and there was music. He closed his eyes and opened them again to see the lights afresh and to swoon again in the soft Lydian airs. He would no doubt have remained in this way fixed and transported (a state possible only on Olympus and hence called the Olympian trance) had not an unexpected thing happened. The lights went out, the fountains stopped playing, and the music ceased. He peered into the darkness. He heard an owl. And then, happily, the lights of the palace shone through the high windows set back among the pillars. It was lovely, a palace fit for the gods, if there should be any here. He tried to get a better look, brushing aside a stubborn branch, and it whipped him across the face. That brought him to, and he realized that if he were to accomplish his mission, now was the time.

He crept out of the opening, and arranged the branches to conceal it. Then he stood still and surveyed the scene. "If there are inhabitants here," he meditated, "and there must be—why otherwise the lights?— surely they are in the palace or they are having supper on the patio." Why this occurred to him he never could figure out. It must have been an inspiration, as we shall soon see, though there seems at this late date little reason to speak so extravagantly about a subordinate hypothesis such as this. And then he began to move. You cannot have verification in a situation like this without moving. He approached the grand stairway, built of the earliest Pleistocene marble, and felt it with his fingers. It was smooth as glacia-lacustrine. He marveled. "How did they ever get that up here?" he asked himself. Then suddenly, looking up towards the top of the stairs, he saw on the other side of the great open doors, made of solid gold, each weighing two tons, a chandelier such as he had never seen before, "a heaven-tree of stars," gleaming in the vaulted ceiling and lighting the grand hall that shone with counter-gleaming. He walked through the doorway. He saw no one, not even a Nubian slave. That would not have surprised him. He tiptoed about. He heard no one. It was very still. He looked about him and caught his reflection in a mirror. The hall was lined with mirrors. "The creatures that inhabit this place must be very beautiful," he said, "otherwise why should they have so many mirrors?" It never occurred to him that human beings of some fantastically higher sort or noble giants or exalted gods would spend time before such mirrors primping or arranging the folds of gorgeous mantels woven of the finest Penelope cloth. And he was right. He leaped before the mirrors to stir them with leaping fire. Suddenly he stopped. Had he seen a great shadow move across the wall? No, there was nothing. He took out his silver flute and played five notes. A unicorn passed by, looked in, and shook its head. "That's strange," he said. But no sound of voice or musical instrument responded to his five notes. He called just a call as school boys do in his native city, the Abdera shrill. Once again there was no answer. The unicorn walked slowly away. "No one here," he said, and he walked back to the doorway to look for the bell. There was no bell. He kicked the door hoping to rouse someone in that way, but one cannot make a noise kicking a golden door. He gave up.

And then it occurred to him, "The Patio! The Patio!" And he bounded down the steps and walked hurriedly around the palace until he came to an ilex tree that stood high above a pool around which, lying on couches and walking or standing, the inhabitants of that great empty palace were now assembled.

He stood now under the ilex tree—and fixed his eyes on the scene below. It was dazzling, so bright. The colors were brighter and the outlines were sharp and clear. He thought of Aldous Huxley and mescaline. And then it suddenly struck him that he could not possibly think of Aldous Huxley and mescaline since neither of these had been invented yet. He looked again, rubbed his eyes, and realized that he now stood on

Mount Olympus and that the air and the times were not the same as those below the mountain. He tried to look into the past and into the future, but no more either of past or future flew in. And then he settled down like a good mortal to survey the scene. He tried to calculate the extent of the pool. But as soon as he settled upon some figure such as two and one-half hectares, the pool would visibly lengthen or shorten, and he would wait for the pool to make up its mind. It did not. He soon made up his mind that there were built-in frustrations against any spying mortal who might want later to report, "It is exactly so." And he gave up. He tried, too, to count the gods and goddesses, but here, too, he failed. Zeus, however, he identified. And that was what he wanted most of all to do.

So the brother of Xenophanes has indeed verified that, as these citizens said, there are, not men, not giants, not Titans, not hemi-demi-semi-gods, but well, whatever they are, gathered round that pool, laughing and jesting and romping as they never would have done had they known that Xenophanes or Plato was standing there under the ilex tree. But were they gods, that is, were they immortals? Well, yes. Had he not seen them pass "the bowl of cherries," as they jokingly referred to the nectar bowl? Of course, he had seen them then, quaffing and laughing. (By the way, did Plato say that the gods did not laugh or that they did not laugh boistrously or only that in human company they should behave more sedately?) And then, of course, there was the huge table laid out with ambrosia in the form of a most royal wedding cake, layer upon layer, mounted with two figures, one of a swan, sweetly remembered of Zeus and the other of a heifer, most sweetly remembered of Hera, "of the white arms." It was quite obvious from this who were in command and who designed the cake in this gathering. Xenophaneses was satisfied. Indeed, he had spied upon the immortals. For see: who drink nectar and eat ambrosia? Are not these the drink and the food of immortals and not of mortals? Hence, too, the famous Greek fear of eating mushrooms and of drinking any liquid with foam on it, for might not the penalty of such eating and drinking be an immortality which, as Jonathan Swift in a later time reminded us, might not be desirable?

Xenophaneses lingered by the ilex tree. He was now obviously waiting for something to happen. It occurred to him (He had heard of scientific explorations and of the notes King Minos had made at the time that he had gone off on a safari and returned home with an oversized bull which he later housed in the library of Crete from which he had for this purpose removed all the books. He figured the bull could not read) in any case it occurred to him to take notes, but the truth of the matter is that he could not write. Besides he wanted to look. However it turned out to be a tame affair. Nothing unseemly happened, and he became impatient to return to the city. But before he left, he took out his hunting blade, a rather primitive version of our jackknife, though for those days a really up-to-date piece of steel with a hinge and shield; and he carved his name on the ilex tree. That, in 1963, is reminiscent, though at this time (some years before Pericles) it could not have been, of that explorer, Perry or Cook, who raised as an extension of the North Pole another pole raised high above the earth to show passers-by who might be slowed up in the snow that, as the saying among scientific explorers goes, Kilroy was here. No doubt Xenophaneses had something of the same sort in mind. He brushed out the chips from his engraving and stood for a moment admiring both his handiwork and his name. It might come in handy should he at some later time come upon unbelievers who, like himself, should ask, "And have you ever been on Olympus?" Then he could say, "Yes, I have," and he could tell them about the ilex tree and about his name there in large letters, in which, as Plato learned, and who knows, perhaps from this very carving, there is a special advantage. They are easier to read. So he left, the tireless gods still around the pool in quiet talk nibbling away at the ambrosia on the table, now leaning like Pisa from too much nibbling on the south side.

He was well satisfied. He had seen for himself. He had verified. "What! No Zeus? Don't be silly. I've been there." And he was not sorry he had gone to all this trouble. His arm still ached from wielding that hatchet. Verification is not easy.

So he returned to the city. It was still dark and the market place was deserted. All the chess tables were empty. He crossed over by way of Ajax lane to Agamemnon Boulevard and so home. He was in high spirits. Tired as he was, physically that is, he did not immediately "hit the straw." This expression, which was in common use in those days, quite different from our own "hit the hay," has in recent years been regarded as reflecting the state of the economy of that time, the popularity of straw indicating—it is or was one of the indicators—a dearth of something, most likely a prolonged drought, and so a preponderence of straw over hay. Instead he took from his bag of books, which he had carried all the way from Lesbos, having changed to another boat there, his precious copy of Homer. He read and read until dawn, and then he went to sleep. He read now with a new zest. He had never found Homer so interesting. For hadn't he seen some of the chief actors in this history? And in the course of his reading, at one of the most exciting moments, it suddenly occurred to him that while he was standing alongside that ilex tree he had not taken notice of any other names carved in the bark. Surely Homer's must have been there. Still Homer might not have carried a knife. Blind as he was he might have had little use for a knife. Still Xenophaneses wished he had looked. And he wondered. Had there been interviews? How did Homer find out all these things? Did the gods keep archives and did Homer have privileged access? The palace was very large and there was room surely for many volumes. How he longed to know whether Homer, too, perhaps before he was blind, had climbed Olympus and fought his way through that wall, that green wall, hawthorn and ivy and creepers and wild plum and barberry immensus. Tomorrow he would think of it again. He had acquired a taste for verification.

When Xenophaneses woke the next morning he was excited. He had seen Zeus and the company of immortals. And now he glanced at the book alongside the straw and remembered some of the things he had read concerning what they had done. He remembered, too, how when he had gone up the mountain he would hardly have conceded, "Well, maybe," and when he had come down he had said, "It is so"—and he hungered for "It is so." But as his expedition to Mount Olympus showed, it was not an easy "It is so" he wanted. He would pay with cuts and bruises if need be. And in spite of his respect for the authority of Homer—it was in the air in Athens—he kept asking such questions as, "And did Zeus do that?" "And did Zeus say that?" And as he said later in discussing such matters with his philosophical friends, one detail that continued to haunt him was that Zeus was only ten feet tall. It was past noon in Athens as he lay on his straw, thinking—and he remembered now too that someone of the few golden men would at some future time say that thinking is the soul in conversation with itself—and listening to the clamor of metal chipping marble on the hill just above his modest diggings. And he got up.

First he ate breakfast, "a grand spread of loaves and cakes on fresh leaves," with wine of course. He also ate "olives and cheese and a country stew of roots and vegetables." There was also a bowl of figs and acorns. The "peas-and-beans" man was late today. He ate with relish. You can't expect to do the work of verification without eating well. He had tried that once in Melos and found out nothing except that you have to eat to verify. "No mastication, no verification," he said with an acorn in his mouth. When he had finished his breakfast he pulled out the stump he sat on, set it against the wall, and took up his writing board and his copy of Homer. He had work to do. He was to be the author of a verified theology. First, he had to assemble what he described as theological propositions. After that would come verification. So he set out to do what any intelligent man of that century or the twentieth would do. He culled from the first book of Homer a list of sentences which, as he supposed, would furnish a test of the possibilities. He was in high spirits. Hadn't he climbed Olympus and seen for himself?

And here now is a list of the sentences he culled. Most of them, as you might expect, are sentences about Zeus.

"And so the counsel of Zeus wrought out its accomplishment."

"Now may the gods that dwell in the mansions of Olympus grant you to lay waste the city of Priam, and to fare happily homeward."

"So spake he in prayer and Phoebus Apollo heard him and came down from the peak of Olympus wroth at heart, bearing on his shoulders his bow and covered quiver. . . ."

"For in his mind did goddess Hera of the white arms put the thought. . . ."

"Seeing that a dream too is of Zeus."

"By his soothsaying that Phoebus Apollo bestowed on him."

"If ever Zeus grant us to sack some well-walled town of Troy."

"I have others by my side that should do me honor, and above all Zeus, lord of counsel."

"Athena came to him from heaven, sent forth of the white-armed goddess, Hera, whose heart loved both alike and had care for them."

"Whosoever obeyeth the gods, to him they hearken gladly."

"Even they that by Zeus's commands watch over the traditions."

"Seeing that no common honor pertaineth to a sceptred king to whom Zeus apportioneth glory."

"Even Zeus that thundereth on high."

"To Zeus whose joy is in the thunder."

"For Zeus went yesterday to Okeanas, unto the noble Ethiopians for a feast."

"Father Zeus, . . . do honor to my son; . . . grant thou victory to the Trojans. . . . Do my son honor and exalt him with recompense."

"But Zeus, the Cloud-Gatherer, said no word to her and sat a long time in silence."

"Then Zeus, the cloud-gatherer, sore troubled, spake to her: 'Verily it is a sorry matter if thou wilt set me at variance with Hera when'er she provoketh me with taunting words.'"

"Kronion spake and bowed his dark brow, and the ambrosial locks waved from the King's immortal head; and he made great Olympus quake."

"Then the father of gods and men made answer to her: 'Hera, think not thou to know all my sayings; hard they are for thee, even though thou art my wife.'"

"Most dread, son of Kronos."

"The Olympian, lord of lightning."

"And laughter unquenchable arose amid the blessed gods to see Hephaestus bustling through the palace."

After he had made his list he sat back on the stump, his back against the wall—he had heard that a verificator should ponder the possibilities for verification in a relaxed position thereby allowing the mind a maximum of inflation—and he read through the list. Some of them he found exceedingly fascinating, such as these: "For in his mind did goddess Hera of the white arms put the thought . . . ;" and "Seeing that a dream too is of Zeus"; and "By his soothsaying that Phoebus Apollo bestowed on him." He pondered over these. It would be difficult. It would not do to make a general enquiry. He would first of all need to settle upon a certain thought, a certain dream, and a certain, it had better be famous, case of soothsaying—in the event he wanted later to publish his results in the Pantheon Press. Finding the certain thought, etc., could be done, though it would be more work. And then what? He had climbed Olympus once and he could do it again. The path was still open. And he thought of himself leaping down those marble steps inlaid with gold, from the ilex tree to the poolside, tapping the goddess Hera of the white arms on the shoulder, at least two feet above him, and saying, "Your Majesty, would you verify for me a little matter that you know all about? Mortals are mortal but they are very curious." He thought he would find the goddess Hera helpful and easy to talk to. Then he would get it settled about Hera's putting a thought into someone's mind. He did not think he could verify that short of asking Hera herself. If she wouldn't tell, he wouldn't find out. It never occurred to him that he would not be welcome. "The poor innocent babe!" He would more likely be whisked off on a cloud, quicker than he could say, "Your Majesty," and dropped like rain alongside some little boat in the Piraeus—or cast head-first into the pool and come up somewhere in the Aegean. When, however, he came now to think of himself approaching Phoebus Apollo to ask him about the most recent phenomenon of soothsaying, and wanting to know whether he, Phoebus Apollo, "Your Honor," was responsible, he suddenly thought of that bow and covered quiver full of arrows, and he felt a hot stinging in his well-rounded thigh. Five minutes later, recovered, he thought of himself walking down those marble steps on tiptoe, bowing and paying his respects as he went, and stopping before the throne, and addressing Zeus, as though Zeus were some genial lover of science and founder of the Institute for Less Mystery, "I hope I am not interrupting anything important but concerning dreams now, could you give us the authentic lowdown?" He hadn't even planned on a nod from the throne before speaking, which shows at once that he did not go to a parochial school or, as they were called in those days, the Olympics. But he soon recovered. He remembered the line "To Zeus whose joy is in the thunder," and he frowned as he thought of "The Cloud-gatherer," "his dark brow," and the "ambrosial locks." He was overwhelmed. He would try something easier first, something on the fringes. The most interesting things would have to come later.

Years after this, at a meeting of the P. L. B., the Pan-Hellenic Learning Bust, an annual affair at which the feasters eat each other's work, he confided to fellow-ravishers that at the time he was considering his confrontations with the Makers of Fact or the News, on Mount Olympus, the difficulty that bothered him most was not the matter of protocol but that of language. It wasn't that, as he anticipated, they, the interviewed divinities, would not understand him—they are adept in understanding four-hundred and twenty-six languages—but that he would not understand them. For it seemed to him likely that they would speak to him in the language to which they were accustomed—the oldest language spoken anywhere, in fact, the original language. He had, as a matter of fact, undertaken the study of the language, which among mortals is said to approximate it most nearly, namely Frisian, but about that time there was an earthquake and he gave it up. Apart from our interest in the subject matter of the fragment, it shows us something of the character of the meetings of the well-learned long ago.

As I hinted earlier, after due consideration, Xenophaneses decided that, however much he would like to know some things, he did not think that, young as he was, it would be wise to risk the lightning on Mount Olympus. The ilex tree was as far as he would go. For the present he was resigned to investigating matters on what he modestly referred to as "on the fringes." The two sentences which struck him then as easily amenable to what he lovingly described as "scientific method" were these: "For Zeus went yesterday to Okeanos, unto the noble Ethiopians for a feast," and "Kronian spake and bowed his dark brow, and the ambrosial locks waved from the King's immortal head; and he made great Olympus quake." It amazed him that Zeus "made great Olympus quake." And this he set about to investigate first.

It was well known in the city that there were occasions on which great Olympus quakes. There had been at least two of these during the last thirty years. On one occasion, on which some people who remembered said that the mountain had shuddered in what they said were quite distinct tantrums or trauma—there were a series of these—a great bundle of shrubbery had come down the mountainside and buried a horse, that, frightened as it then was, came dragging a mound of blueberry bushes into the marketplace. That quake was remembered thereafter as the blueberry quake. On another occasion, after an unusual tremor, about a half hour after the tremor, what the natives described as a huge dishpan with the initial *H* engraved on the rim came tumbling and banging and bouncing down the rocky slope. That half-hour interval had often been referred to as a measure of the height of Olympus. But the letter *H*, which I have already said was taken to be an initial, had aroused more speculation. Was it, as some said, "H stands for Hera," from whose kitchen it had no doubt been hurtle-turtled, or as others said, "H stands for Hephaestus," whose handiwork it certainly was. At any rate these details still fresh in the popular memory were enough to convince Xenophaneses that indeed great Olympus did quake. There were in those days no public records, no seismographs. In fact, weather reports and weather forecasts did not come into the Athenian press until about six hundred B.C. It was, however, said that at the time of the last quake the water splashed so high along the boardwalk on the waterfront near the fishmarket that women shopping there were drenched and some lost their fish.

So that there had been quakes was well authenticated. Xenophaneses wished that tomorrow there might be another quake, but there would, as he well knew, have been no point to that. The question was as to whether Zeus made the quake—and concerning this, the people whom he met in the gymnasium where he went to interview citizens were not of much help. Some said, "Of course, Zeus did," but when Xenophaneses pressed them a bit they said, "We've always known that," or, "Tiresias told my father." Only one of them said that he had read it in Homer. It seems that what they called their scriptures were not much read; not, of course, that it would have been any help to Xenophaneses. Others said, "Zeus? Why should Zeus make the mountain quake? He has other things to do, such as pure thinking." One young man was not very nice and snorted, and began, "Zeus, if there is a Zeus, but there is no Zeus," and Xenophaneses, who was now thirty-five-years old, an older man, really laid him out and called him a whippersnapper and rebuked him for such irresponsible talk. "Go," he said, "and climb Olympus and look down from the ilex tree before you throw in your fifty cents that isn't worth two." (This expression "your fifty cents that isn't worth two" had come in recently with the new coinage in which the drachma was withdrawn. The reform, however, did not last and so the expression also went out.) Without the expense or verification he never could or would have spoken with such authority. Rumor has it that that young man later joined Xenophaneses in his investigations and was responsible for several of the experimental devices which played so important a role in the advance of theological science.

When Xenophaneses sought more detail among those who said, "Of course, Zeus did," asking how Zeus did this, there were, as he came to see, two factions. There were those who said that Zeus did this by waving his ambrosial locks. These called themselves the orthodox adelphies. The other group, of a more rationalist bent, did not, as they said, understand how Zeus could do this by waving his ambrosial locks. They were careful to insist that Zeus did indeed wave his ambrosial locks. They did not want to deny that. But they said that Zeus made great Olympus shake by stamping his foot. One can readily see in this suggestion anticipations of that later controversy among theoreticians as to whether a cause causing one can cause an effect without said cause being in juxta-contact with the what in which the caused effect inheres. Xenophaneses was inclined to the stamp-foot view, a view also more popular among the younger citizens. What surprised him, however, most of all was that no one among those he asked, held the view, later publicized by Archimedes in a lecture written on a wall, to the effect that Zeus had made great Olympus shake, not by waving his ambrosial locks, nor by stamping his foot, but by the use of a lever. Archimedes, as we now know, never did climb Olympus, and this may account for what we cannot but regard as an anthropomorphism.

Xenophaneses, at the end of a month, was convinced that if he were to investigate this matter and once and for all settle the issue, he would have to ascend Olympus once more. But when? Naturally, it would be best to do this on the day or night before the quake in order to be in a position to observe Zeus, especially during the five minutes just preceding the quake. He would watch then to see whether Zeus shook his ambrosial locks and then, or stamped his foot and then, or whether he sank his crowbar into the side of the mountain and shook it and then, or something else. What if Zeus only coughed; would Xenophaneses be ready for the quake and make the proper connections? He thought of that and hoped he would be ready. He made his preparations and waited for the day before the day of the next quake. Which day was that? For that information he consulted the astrologers. They all agreed. It would be the sixth of the seventh. On the fifth of the seventh he ascended the mountain and took his place under the ilex tree. Five minutes before the quake—his hourglass had sprung a leak—he took out his knife to smooth out an irregularity in the carving of his name in the bank of the tree. And while he was busy the quake came and he was knocked off his feet and fell face forward in a bed of ripe strawberries. He had missed. There would not be another quake in fifteen years.

He went down the mountain disappointed. Along the way he flung the hourglass from him and it was shattered on a stone. "You're an anachronism anyhow," he shouted after it. He forgot that on Olympus there are no anachronisms. When he got home he wrote an account of his adventure in order that the future of verification might not lose the benefit of his effort. His own adventure he described as one of weak verification due to sand, quicksand, too quick for the hourglass. It never occurred to him that, not quicksand, but vanity was the condition which led to his having his eyes fixed on his own good name in the bark of the tree when they should have been fixed on Zeus who made Great Olympus shake, not by waving his ambrosial locks, nor by stamping his foot, nor by a crowbar, nor by a cough, but in his own sweet way.

Xenophaneses was tired. He rested the next day, it was the seventh of the seventh and he always rested on the seventh. On the eighth of the seventh he went fishing. He had no luck. He didn't mind. He watched the minnows. For hours not a theological proposition went through his mind. But on the fourteenth of the seventh, after one-hundred-and-two nibbles, there it was: "For Zeus went yesterday to Okeanos, unto the noble Ethiopians for feast." Now did he, Zeus, do that? He would find out. He would vindicate Homer. And he did. He first sent letters to the Ras Selah who invited him to visit him in the city of Addis Ali Baba, saying that indeed Zeus had visited us, noble Ethiopians, and would he like to inspect the banquet hall where Zeus (on a public relations jaunt) and the chieftains had feasted for a fortnight and perhaps had eaten more than was good for their figures. The hall had been preserved in memory of that occasion, and there was still a mound outside the silver door in the rear where the leavings of the feast had been carried in order to tempt the flies away from the tables while Ras Selas and the chieftains—horsemen and hurlers of the spear who put on a show for their guest—and the Grand Thunderer and Cloud-Gatherer sat down to drink dark red wine. He went. And this time he kept to his business. His business? Verification. He saw the hall and he saw the mound.

An Introduction to Nietzsche's Letters

This paper was written in 1968 as an introduction to a proposed volume of Nietzsche's letters translated by Christopher Middleton. The paper, however, stands alone. The volume was to be part of a Nietzsche series edited by William Arrowsmith and John Silber and published by the University of Chicago Press. When Bouwsma submitted his introduction, the director of the press took a very negative view of it and rejected the whole introduction. In strong disagreement, Arrowsmith and Silber resigned as editors of the series and the introduction was never published. Middleton's translation was subsequently published with the title *Selected Letters of Friedrich Nietzsche* (University of Chicago Press, 1969). The quotations from Nietzsche's letters are all taken from the unpublished typescript of Middleton's book; therefore, indented quotations are not footnoted.

Anyone who writes an introduction is somewhat like a doorman who meets visitors at the door to open the door for them, to invite them in, even to guide them through a few rooms to give them a taste of what they may find in other rooms. Naturally what rooms he shows will depend on the interest of the visitors. I should add that the doorman is familiar with the house and has some opinions about the house generally, has overheard some visitors comment on what they have seen, and he may have had some thoughts too about the builder of this house, even about the people who live in it now. Of course, he is no authority. He is only a doorman.

And so it is, learning from the doorman, I am to write an introduction to this translation of a collection of Nietzsche's letters. In doing so, I am to open the book to prospective readers and to say, "Look at this," "Read this." But what I ask any man to look at must be suited to the interest of that reader. What sort of readers are there? There are some who will enjoy reading distinguished prose. For them I am prepared to quote aphorisms, "Listen to this." There are others who will read to satisfy their curiosity about this man. There are his relations with women, with Richard Wagner, with his sister and mother, with his friends, with Germans. There is material enough in these letters to help them to understand this man who presumably understood himself so well. There may be other readers who are like "the Athenians and strangers which were there, (who) spent their time in nothing else but either to tell or to hear some new thing."

I am going on now to quote a few aphorisms such as one may find scattered throughout these letters, scattered like previous stones. But those who are interested in distinguished prose may also be interested in a few passages in which Nietzsche is reflecting on his style, for Nietzsche is a self-conscious writer. But first to the aphorisms. The temptation will be to go on quoting, but I will restrain myself.

> Who would refute a phrase of Beethoven or who would find error in Raphael's Madonna?
> Truth seldom dwells where people have built temples for it and have ordained priests.
> One is honest about oneself either with a sense of shame or vanity.
> Every sick man is a rascal . . . and what a host of sicknesses there are.
> Definitely the most horrible thing is doubt with its ghostly half reality.
> All fathers are clumsy.
> It is certainly not dissipation to read a good book each year.
> Become the being you are.
> Some people are born posthumously.
> To be a Christian . . . will hereafter be improper.
> I treat all the German philosophers as unconscious counterfeiters.
> There is in me a distrust of dialectic, of reason.

I said that I would restrain myself.

Now for some of those reflections on his own style. Anyone who has tried to write well or who would like to try will be struck by them. Here, by the way, is another aphorism: "No man has a good style by nature." These are the passages:

Early in his career, when Nietzsche was twenty-three, he wrote to a friend of his:

> The scales are falling from my eyes; I lived all too long in a state of stylistic innocence. The categorical imperative 'Thou shalt and must write' has aroused me. I tried, that is, something that I had never tried except at school: to write well, and suddenly the pen froze in my hand. I could not do it and was annoyed. And all the while Lessing's and Lichtenberg's and Schopenhauer's stylistic precepts were buzzing in my ears. It was always my solace that these three authorities unanimously agreed that it is difficult to write well, that no man has a good style by nature, that one must work at the up-hill job of acquiring one. I honestly do not want to write again so woodenly and dryly, in such a logical

corset, as I did. . . . Above all a few gay spirits in my own style must once more be unchained, I must learn to play on them as on a keyboard, but not only pieces I have learned by heart, no, free fantasies, as free as possible, yet still always logical and beautiful.

But when the time comes I shall impress myself with as much seriousness and freedom of mind as possible. Knowledge, art, and philosophy are growing into each other so much in me, that I shall in any case give birth to a centaur.

It is my theory that with this Zarathustra, I have brought the German language to a state of perfection. After Luther and Goethe, a third step had to be taken;—look and see, old chum of mine, if vigor, flexibility, and euphony have ever consented as well in our language. Read Goethe after reading a page of my book—and you will feel that that 'undulatory' quality peculiar to Goethe as a draughtsman was not foreign to the shape of language also. My line is superior in strength and manliness without becoming, as Luther's did, loutish. My style is a dance; a play of symmetries of every kind, and an overleaping and mockery of these symmetries. This enters the very vowels.

I am not going to quote anything for those who are interested especially in Nietzsche's personal relationships. In reading some of these letters I have at times been reminded of a sentence from Tolstoy's *War and Peace:* "Rostov . . . learned that Dolohov, this bully, this noted duellist Dolohov, lived at Moscow with his old mother and a hunchback sister, and was *the tenderest son and brother.*" I want to avoid the impression that Nietzsche was a bully, but he was hard and for years "the tenderest son and brother." He wrote, "Be hard . . . treat precisely what is most hostile to me with the greatest gentleness (which) involves danger, not only for me but also for my task; and it is here that the hardening is necessary, and with a view to educating others, and occasional cruelty." The same Nietzsche who made such "an outrageous attack on Christianity" was "the tenderest son" to his mother, the widow of a Lutheran minister. Enough.

For those people who will turn to these letters to get help to understand Nietzsche better, a man so occupied with the meaning of his own life: "I would like to be something," "There is a lot of work to do," "Only as fighters have we in our time a right to exist," "the desire to do something properly and well," "I too believe that I represent something holy," "Behind all the daily and perhaps petty work, some embracing and very large project," "the terrifying face of my more distant life task," "I have an aim." To understand such expressions and to suggest some of the promise which these letters afford, I say promise, I am quoting the following.

In a letter to his sister, written when he was twenty-one, a young man, he wrote:

On the other hand, is it really so difficult simply to accept everything in which one has been brought up, which has gradually become deeply rooted in oneself, which goes for true among relatives and among many good people, which does moreover really comfort and elevate man, is that more difficult than *to take new paths, struggling against habituation, uncertain of one's indepen-dent course, amid frequent vacillations of the heart, and even of the con-science, often comfortless, but always pursuing the eternal goal of the true, the beautiful, the good?*
Is it then a matter of acquiring the view of God, world and Atonement in which one can feel most comfortable, is it not rather the case that for the true researchers, the result of his research is of no account at all? Do we in our investigations search for tranquility, peace, happiness? No, only for the truth, even if it were to be frightening and ugly.

He goes on:

Every true faith is indeed infallible, it performs what the believing person hopes to find in it, but it does not offer the least support for the establishing of an objective truth.
Here the ways of men divide: if you want to achieve peace of mind and happiness, then have faith, if you want to be a disciple of truth, then search.

In concluding this part of the letter, he writes: "On this earnest foundation I shall now build—and the building will be all the jollier."
This resolve, "I shall now build," Nietzsche made when he was young. What is most interesting for our purpose is that it is a resolve. And to understand Nietzsche may be thought of as understanding that resolve both in terms of this statement of it and in terms of the ensuing life which was the keeping of it. This is, of course, only the beginning. The keeping of this resolve is a continuing engagement with the condi-tions under which it is to be kept and the articulation of that resolve as those conditions changed. Nietzsche is a self-conscious worker, reflect-ing both upon "his intentions and aims" and upon the high cost in terms of "peace of mind and happiness," in terms of relatives and many good people. And he continually fortifies himself with new resolution.
To suggest how that resolution developed throughout the years, here is another quotation from another letter written toward the end of his letter-writing—also to his sister:

The task which is imposed upon me is all the same my nature—so that only now do I comprehend what was my predestined good fortune. I play with the burden which would crush any other mortal . . . for what I have to do is *terrible*, in any sense of the word; I do not challenge individuals, I am challenging humanity as a whole with my terrible accusation; which ever way the decision may go, for me or against me, in any case, there attaches to my name a quantity of doom that is beyond telling.

From the same letter, "I hold quite literally, the future of mankind in the palm of my hand."

Is this the resolve—"and the building will be all the jollier"—of that earlier letter, and has it grown now to such proportions as to make of that earnest young man a monster? (What a pity about that handsome frog—"hath yet a jewel in its head"—that blew itself to bits—"I, too, am dynamite"—in its effort to be as big as the ox.) Kierkegaard had a use on a number of occasions for the following passage from the *Phaedrus*, quoting Socrates: "I do not examine such things but only myself, desiring to know whether I am a monster more complicated and swollen with passion than the serpent Typhon, or a creature of a gentler sort, partaking by nature in something more divine and passionless." Reminded of this I am the more confused. Now I should ask, "Is this the resolve . . . and has it grown now to such proportions as to make of the earnest young man a god?" That would make of my outbreak of pity for the frog a form of blasphemy. Besides would one dare to pity in the presence of Nietzsche?

Above I introduced the question, What was Nietzsche trying to do? I have now borrowed if not intelligible statements of what he was trying to do, intimations of something very big indeed. Early we get the expressions "to take new paths," "pursuing the eternal goal of the true, the beautiful, the good," "search," "investigation." In this earlier statement there is considerable naiveté. The young man can still write of the true, the beautiful, the good. All that is changed is the order. The good comes last. In the later statement there is "the burden which would crush any other mortal," "what I have to do is terrible," "my terrible accusation," "a quantity of doom that is beyond telling." If someone were to ask what those new paths are, how he is to pursue "the eternal goal," how "the search" is carried on, perhaps someone could answer, and one might say that the books and the letters show us what all these things are. And so too with "the terrible accusations," "the burden," "the quantity of doom." Should I say that the future of mankind that he held in his hand is what we have in 1969 or "Look we for another," doom?

And here is an excerpt from one of the earlier letters, prophetic of what is to come:

Three things are my relaxations, but infrequent ones: my Schopenhauer, Schumann's music, and then solitary walks. Yesterday a magnificent storm was in the sky. I hurried out to a nearby hilltop, called "Leusch" (perhaps you can tell me what that means), found a hut up there, a man who was slaughtering two kids, and his young son. The storm broke with immense force, with wind and hail. I felt an incomparable elation, and I know for certain that we can understand nature aright when we have to run to her, away from our troubles and pressures. What to me was man and his unquiet will! What was the eternal "Thou shalt," "Thou shalt not"! How different the lightning, the wind, the hail, free powers, without ethics! How fortunate, how strong they are, pure will, without obscurings from the intellect.

Who knows? That elation, those "free powers" in that storm, may well have provided him with that "lifelong task," that of restoring to human life the purity of the lightning and the wind which are neither troubled by nor obey "Thou shalt" or "Thou shalt not," "without ethics."

For the "Athenians and strangers" I have reserved these paragraphs:

If you should ever come round to writing about me, . . . be sensible enough . . . to characterize me, to "describe"—but not to evaluate. . . . I have never been characterized, either as a psychologist or as a writer (including poet), or as the inventor of a new kind of pessimism (a Dionysian pessimism born of strength, which takes pleasure in seizing the problem of existence by the horns), or as an Immoralist the highest form, till now, of "intellectual rectitude" which is permitted to treat morality as illusion, having itself become instinct and inevitability.

Would that others had the gifts to see ourselves, not as others see us, but as we, ourselves, see us: Psychologist, Writer, Neo-Pessimist, Immoralist.

For those Athenians who have read Plato and Saint Augustine, the following shockers may serve to provide a jolt:

This variety includes my blue fingers, as usual, my black thoughts. . . . The falsifying of everything actual by morality stands there in fullest array: wretched psychology.—And it is all Plato's fault! He is still Europe's greatest misfortune.

If Nietzsche wrote this on Monday, he might well have scratched it out on Tuesday. But there is no doubt about its transvaluation of a current value on Monday. I did not say that Nietzsche would scratch it out on Tuesday.

I am going on to another shocker. There is a passage in the *Notes from the Underground* which goes, "Now when I am not only recalling them (early adventures) but have actually decided to write an account of them, I want to try the experiment whether one can, even with oneself, be perfectly open and not take fright at the whole truth. I will observe, in parenthesis, that Heine says that a true autobiography is almost an impossibility, and that man is bound to lie about himself. He considers that Rousseau certainly told lies about himself in his confessions, and even intentionally lied, out of vanity." I had a friend [Yorick Smythies] who, in commenting on that passage, said that there was one man who wrote about himself and did not lie. That man was Saint Augustine. There were special reasons for this. He wrote about himself, confessing, not as Rousseau did, to anyone who would care to read, but to God, "who seeth the heart" and to whom one cannot lie. It was accordingly with this back in my mind that I came upon the following passage in Nietzsche. It was pretty much like a slap in the face. Here is the passage:

I have been reading, as relaxation, Saint Augustine's *Confessions*, regretting much that you were not with me. O this old rhetorician! What falseness, what rolling of eyes! How I laughed! (For example, concerning the "theft" of his youth, basically an undergraduate story) what psychological falsity! (For example, when he talks about the death of his best friend with whom he shared a single soul, he resolved to go on living, so that in this "way his friend would not wholly die." Such things are revoltingly dishonest.) Philosophical value zero. Vulgarized Platonism; that is to say, a way of thinking that was invented for the highest aristocracy of soul and which he adjusted to suit slave-natures. Moreover, one sees into the guts of Christianity in this book. I make my observations with the curiosity of a radical physician and physiologist.

I realize that Nietzsche, like Saint Augustine, wrote about himself, though not quite in the same tone of voice, and that some have called out to Diogenes, "Here's your man." Heine said, "Almost an impossibility." I propose another phrase, "almost a possibility." I am presenting a psychologist. I am not evaluating. But all the same one may be slapped in the face by a psychologist. Nietzsche was well aware of that.

The doorman has invited visitors into the house and told them about some of the things they may find there. I did not say that the house is a labyrinth and that one may come upon some surprising things there, a piece on a poem of Hölderlin, pieces on music, on the difference between classical and modern metric. I gave no warning that a Minotaur lived there and that the place is not safe. Children under sixteen? If accompanied by delinquent parents. Especially attractive to authors who are looking for something to say, of whom there have been quite a few. Earlier I remarked of the doorman that he had some familiarity with the house, that he had an ear for comment visitors made as they passed through the door, or stood waiting. The doorman is agreeable. He has little to say. He is only a doorman. He reports only what he has heard, scraps of opinion. These scraps may be more useful in stirring up trouble. In reading these letters one is bound to have thoughts. These scraps are thoughts too and may keep the rumination going. If anyone should get the impression that what follows is a disconnected discourse—with connections—he will get the right impression. Irritants and Counter-Irritants

The Wasteland:

Cracks and reforms and bursts in the violet air
Falling towers
Jerusalem   Athens   Alexandria
Vienna   London
Unreal

These are our home. What are we to do? "What is that noise?" "Do you see nothing? Do you remember nothing?" "What shall I do now? What shall I do?" When the huffing and puffing are over and the dust settles, we shall begin again rolling the stone uphill. That is not Nietzsche. We shall build a new Jerusalem, a new Athens, a new Alexandria, a new Vienna, and a new London. Operation Bootstrap with seven-league boots. We'll not need God or art anymore. We are our own boot makers.

This has been going on a long time, man looking at man, as though seeing him for the first time, each in his own time. High he stands on the mountain looking down, and too, walking among men to look straight into their faces. He was "like unto one of us save that he was without" cowardice. So superior he was. He accused, accused, exhorted, exhorted, cried, "Joe, Joe." He shook us up. He showed us the way or at least half of the way. Then he said, "Now you are on your own." In the field of wheat there may be a stalk of grain that is grain higher than all the rest, distinguished, noble grain, strong, grain above all other grain. He is our hope. "The full grain in the ear." Tomorrow, tomorrow! Tomorrow is the light of today. Or today is the beacon that lights up tomorrow. Hope worketh tribulation and tribulation new resolution, new resolution new strength and new strength new offense. But above all good red meat. Meat is superman.

Isn't there sometimes a little whimper in his letters? Would it be pardonable to hope so?

No one can understand Nietzsche without an appreciation of what made his gorge rise. "All the world is a stage"? Bad acting? No. The world is a hospital and all the men and women are sick. One may not share that nausea, "my gorge rises at it," but one must share in understanding that representation of the world. For the sick, a radical cure. Nietzsche prescribed that cure not only for himself but also for all who are sick and have the strength and will to be cured. Every man must cure himself. Like the doctors in Plato's *Republic* he has himself been sick. So he understands sickness and cure. And from what then do men suffer? From Jesus Christ and from Christianity and from morals. Men are sick in the will.

Karl Barth once denounced "the dreadful, godless, ridiculous opinion that man is the Atlas who is destined to bear the dome of heaven on his shoulders." There, he said, is "the final root and ground of all human disorders."

Freud said, "In my youth he (Nietzsche) signified a nobility to which I could not attain." He (Freud) several times said of Nietzsche that he had a more penetrating knowledge of himself than any other man who ever lived or was ever likely to live.

This was written of Orwell: "The real problem, as he saw it, was to preserve mankind's ethical values—honor, mercy, justice, respect for others—in the face of an almost universal disappearance of a belief in the immortality of the soul. . . . When people ceased to be Christians they did not necessarily become good humanists, but superstitious fanatics and political madmen."

These quotations may remind us that not all disputes are intellectual. One man's ridiculous is another man's noble.

Ecclesiastes: "What profit hath a man. . . . One generation passeth away. . . . The sun also ariseth. . . . The wind goeth towards the south. . . . All the rivers run into the sea. . . . The thing that hath been, it is that which shall be . . . and behold, all is vanity and vexation of spirit. Vanity of vanities all is vanity."

Nietzsche: "What joy, what joy, that 'one generation . . . The sun . . . , The wind . . . , all the rivers . . . , The thing that hath been, it is that which shall be!' What joy!"

Some people may find this difficult. How are we to understand this? If we regard eternal recurrence as a carousel, then the same bright horses and riders and the same organ music may be charming for, let us say, an hour. But in a week the carnival moves on. Ah! but the children! "Except ye become as little children ye cannot enter" into the joy of eternal carousel. Perhaps. On the other hand the transvaluation of values requires transvaluation here, too. For disrelish, new relish. For vexation of spirit, joy. The will to joy will provide.

Nietzsche is more like a man out of a book, a man such as Dostoevsky might have created, a character like Ivan. One would not expect to meet Ivan on the street or even in anyone's home. And even if one did one wouldn't recognize him. He lives in his thoughts. And this is true of Nietzsche. Ivan is a thinker. Nietzsche is a thinker. Ivan did not have the will to believe his thought. Smerdyakov had the will. Ivan furnished the thought. When this happened, Ivan was shocked into the realization that he was responsible for both the thought and the will. If a man thinks murder and then the murder takes place, what then? Nietzsche, like Ivan, writes and writes and writes. He writes dynamite. "All things are lawful." Were what he wrote to explode, as what Ivan wrote and spoke exploded in the person of Smerdyakov, what then should we expect? Had there been no Smerdyakov, Ivan's talk might have been passed off as clever and mildly shocking. Smerdyakov misunderstood or understood so well that he showed Ivan what he was saying. Some people think they know who it was understood Nietzsche as Smerdyakov understood Ivan.

I asked a man well read, well studied in Nietzsche, what the lifelong task was. He could not say. He had only read and studied and loved Nietzsche's books. I asked him, And what did Nietzsche do to you? I had in mind Nietzsche, the explosive, the dynamite. The question surprised him. Had Nietzsche not changed his life? He was bewildered. He was well read, well studied, and he loved Nietzsche's books. Kierkegaard predicted of his own books that they would be well read, well studied, and searched and researched. I do not know that he said that they would be loved. But by whom well read, well studied? By scholars who would find it interesting to tell other scholars who could not read what Kierkegaard meant by this comma and that omitted word. And so Kierkegaard's work, written for another purpose, would serve the paragraph pickers. How otherwise would a privat-dozent ever get to be a professor? Neither Kierkegaard nor Nietzsche wrote to serve the interests of intellectuals who might then go on to write other books, readable or unreadable. "Of the writing of many books there is no end." We might say that Kierkegaard wrote to shake the unshaken and Nietzsche wrote to spread terror. If irony won't do it, will dynamite? Who in any case wants to be shaken, or who asks for terror. It is safer and more pleasant admiring the art with which these men shake the unshaken and spread terror or try to.

"And lo, thou art unto them as a very lovely song of one that hath a pleasant voice, and can play well on an instrument: for they hear thy words, but they do not do them."

In reading Nietzsche, particularly the letters, we are cautioned that no man who writes about himself is to be trusted. The reason for this is that a man in writing about himself has a motive just as he does when he lies. Frequently, what in such a case he tells is belied by the very fact that he tells it. A man in doing so, as someone said earlier about the writer of the notes, tries to give himself a character, tries to present himself as such and such a person—perhaps even for such and such a purpose. A man wants to be known as. . . . Hence, when we read Nietzsche, for instance, we can see how he is presenting himself, what character he is giving himself, but that is all. What the man is—perhaps in spite of his presentation of himself—must remain a secret. If Nietzsche tells us that the reason he has so few friends is that he is so candid, are we to believe him? And if he tells us quite simply that he is so candid because he is interested in educating others, are we to believe him? If he tells us he is honest—even if he tells the truth—are we to believe him? May he not be concealing the motive for that honesty that makes of his honesty dishonesty? If Nietzsche writes of Saint Augustine, as he does to impress us with his superior truthfulness,—since in writing of Saint Augustine, he makes much of his falsity—may he not, as a matter of fact, want to shock us and show us, too, something original? Above I used the expression "What a man is," but what are we to make of that? It seems that we must distinguish between a man's presenting himself and a man's being himself. And doesn't this presenting oneself enter into a man's life in a large range of his activities? It isn't limited to those episodes in which a man talks or writes about himself. What are you doing?—are you interested in the subject: "Words are signs" or are you, by way of discussing that, presenting yourself as an original and witty and clever person? Even when you begin a discussion in your class or when you read a short story of Tolstoy—both of which may be good to do and both of which you may do very well, does it occur to you, while you are doing these, that what you are doing and how you do it make a favorable impression? And when you say in your note that a letter you received frightened you even though it did, what was your saying that for? Wasn't it to show that you have a striking and original way of expressing yourself? Clearly honesty is not a matter of saying what is true. That is easy enough. The "falsity," "the illogical falsity," consists in one's using one's saying what is true for an altogether different purpose, namely, to present oneself as someone who tells the truth. One can do that by telling the truth as one can work hard in order to present oneself as one who is hardworking. And now we can understand how it may be with Nietzsche. Why is Nietzsche so straightforward, so honest, so courageous? He is presenting himself as straightforward, as honest, as courageous. No man ever watched himself and the effects he made upon people more than Nietzsche did.

There is a man walking. That is simple. There is also a man walking, walking in such a way as to make an impression—perhaps on himself. And there is a man walking, conscious that he is being seen walking, and his way of walking is the judgment of him, and now he makes his walk conform to the judgment he wants. Too bad a man cannot allow what he is naturally to speak for him. He is born to distort. Still, this is hard to understand. It isn't that a man changes his walk to match the judgment he wants. The difference is more subtle. It's as though walking, his walk said, "I am just walking. I am nonchalant." But he isn't. He is also saying, "I am just walking. I am nonchalant." No one expects that double-mindedness to be noticed. But the man who says, "I am nonchalant," has injected nonchalance into the situation, one might say "non-nonchalance" or "chalance." He might better have said, "I, chalant, am now putting on nonchalance."

Doesn't Nietzsche call attention to his impudence, his arrogance, his giving offense, his bravado, at the same time that he puts on an apologetic air for these things? "See how impudent I am! See how haughty I am! You can tell by how ashamed I am." Or is it more like boasting!

And might not a man become what he represents himself to be? If he were to live a thousand years? Perhaps this is where Existentialism fails. If only man had a thousand years!

Dostoevsky wrote the *Brothers Karamazov* in 1881. This was the same year in which Nietzsche wrote to his friend Peter Gast, "Ah, my friend, sometimes the idea runs through my head that I am living an extremely dangerous life, for I am one of those machines that can explode. The intensities of my feelings make me shudder and laugh,—several times I could not leave my room for the ridiculous reason that my eyes were inflamed—from what? Each time I had wept too much on my previous day's walk, not sentimental tears but tears of joy; I sang and talked nonsense, filled with a glimpse of things which put me in advance of all other men."

In advance of all other men and in advance, too, of Ivan! Miosov gives the following report of Ivan: "Only five days ago, in a gathering here, principally of ladies, he solemnly declared in argument that there was nothing in the whole world to make men love their neighbors. That there was no law of nature that man should love mankind, and that if there had been any law on earth hitherto, it was not owing to a natural law, but simply because men have believed in immortality. Ivan Fyodorovitch added in parenthesis that the whole natural law lies in that faith, and that if you were to destroy in mankind the belief in immortality, not only love, but every living force maintaining the life of the world would at once be dried up. Moreover nothing then would be immoral, everything would be lawful, even cannibalism. That's not all. He ended by asserting that for every individual like ourselves who does not believe in God or immortality the moral law of nature must immediately be changed into the exact contrary of the former religious law, and that egoism, even to crime must become, not only lawful, but even recognized as the inevitable, the most rational, and even honorable outcome of his position."

Nietzsche and Ivan agree in this "the moral law of nature must immediately be changed into the exact contrary of the former religious law." And then? They both weep, the one "sentimental tears," the other "tears of joy." So the issue is one of what we are to weep at and what tears—scarcely an intellectual one.

Neither Kierkegaard nor Nietzsche brought about the situation which was the occasion of their work. In their work they brought to the attention of men who had no eyes, no ears for such things, what had taken place. From then on people saw it. According to Kierkegaard, a gigantic misunderstanding had denied men the challenge, the venture of faith. When men do not understand they cannot choose. "Choose ye this day." Nietzsche had a more dramatic way of announcing to the world what he had noticed—and willed—namely, "God is dead." He might also have announced, Man is dead, and then proclaimed a resurrection.

What is that I hear? A voice crying in the wilderness of Copenhagen. A voice crying? No, a voice lecturing.

Think of Nietzsche as a storm, thunder and lightning and wind, a natural force, a tornado, ruthless, tearing away at the landscape, spreading ruin. "I have come not to bring peace," but ruin. A self-conscious storm, a wonder, a spectacle, the rebel Satan "going to and fro upon the earth seeking that which he might devour." "It is my nature."

Voltaire said, "If there is no God it will be necessary to invent him," which is much like saying, "Better leave things as they are. We have invented God already." But Nietzsche said, If there is no God, it is high time we were getting rid of him.

Someone whose name I cannot spell said that you could find in Nietzsche a parody of Christianity. And in explanation of this he quoted the following passage from one of the early letters:

The most important thing for me is that here (Vegetarianism) is another tangible case of that optimism which keeps cropping up in the strangest forms, now as socialism, now as cremation —as opposed to burial, now as vegetarian doctrine, and in countless forms; just as if the removal of a sinfully unnatural phenomenon could mean the establishment of happiness and harmony. Whereas our sublime philosophy teaches that whenever we reach out our hands we grasp total ruin. The pure will to life, and here all palliatives are meaningless.

Where, he asked, did "our sublime philosophy" get that idea? He went on to say that the abstract of Christianity would look very much like that of "our sublime philosophy," only the cast of characters would be different. The roles played would be much the same. I suggested that the stage would have to be turned upside down. I had to admit that that was not clear.

One might be interested in the development of Nietzsche, the awareness dawning on him that he was to assume a task and his continuing progress to that end, his withdrawing from the foolishness and worldliness of other men, steeling himself against their hostility. What did he do? He wrote books. But what was he doing writing books? Did he think he could do what he seems to have set out to do? He did not want to be a literary man or to be known and discussed as a literary man. It is difficult to measure the influence of a man like Nietzsche. How many men has he infuriated? How many men has he inspired to—infuriate? "I can see clearly the task for which I live as a factum of indescribable sadness, but transfigured by my consciousness that there is greatness in it, if ever there was greatness in the task of mortal man." He stepped forward, did not look back, kept on, hurting with each step, deaf to cries, "Stop! Stop!" What was that task? One stands aghast at the enormity of such a conception of one's own life and the frightful seriousness with which this man pursued it—even though one does not understand it.

Nietzsche was to be deficient in nothing in his rivalry with Christianity. If Christians will eat a crocodile, I will do it. If they will drink eisel, I will do it. If they rejoice in suffering in nakedness and cold, I will rejoice in suffering in nakedness and cold. And I will do all this on my own. In this way Nietzsche makes his own peculiar advance on Christianity. It is hard to enjoy suffering, but it can be done if one has the hardier aesthetic sense to match the suffering. Even toothache can be enjoyed. It is like moaning but not "without trills and flourishes." There is victory in that.

Nietzsche is like that North Wind that tried to blow the coat off that man—in a contest with the sun. And the man wrapped that coat about him all the more tightly. But some men lost their coats and were naked. Sartor Resartus. Clothes, clothes, clothes.

Isn't it better to read Nietzsche for the tidbits of exquisite raillery, complaint, pleading, explaining, boasting, exhorting, ridicule, etc.? When a man says he loves Nietzsche's books he is still not telling us what he loves.

Nietzsche understood himself. This is not the same as his knowing what he wanted in the way in which a man might want something and another man or a genie might bring it to him. Nor is it in the way in which a man might want something and then seeing he could not have it might settle for something else. If we say that Nietzsche understood himself then he must understand by this that he conceived of his life in terms of a task. "This one thing I do." He understood himself in the way in which Saint Paul understood himself. But a poet, too, may understand himself. His task? To write poems. His task is shown in what he composes; in his accomplishment. He cannot describe the poem that he is about to write. Is that then how it is with all creators, and did

Nietzsche think of his task in this way? A poet has words, the language is the medium, in which he works. And what is Nietzsche to compose? New souls, new men. This is the task of the Immoralist. He is subject to a task laid on him by "the tyrant, the inexorable tyrant," his "predestined nature," his "inner voices," "life." ("Life has proposed my duty to me.") Can we find among the new souls some of Nietzsche's creations? The categorical imperative is no tyrant. It is, if not sweetly reasonable, reasonable. It answers all questions. But the tyrant is peremptory, answers no questions. "Then the Lord answered Job out of the whirlwind."

(Someone has said that a poem is the answer to a question which cannot be asked, the solution to a problem that cannot be stated.)

Some people understand Socrates. I do not. There is something inhuman about Socrates. He is more like a god, serene, calm, unworried, unafraid. If he is threatened, if he has to drink the hemlock, "the hour is near," he is unperturbed. I am not denying that he is magnificent. He is among the simpleminded. He has this one thing to do, a task, imposed upon him by God, the inner voice. His task is to go about conversing with people, getting them to see that they do not understand what they are saying. It is a thankless and dangerous task. He is not afraid. In a god that is not surprising. No one can hurt a god. Nietzsche in much the same way I do not understand. That a god should undertake what to me seems fantastic should cause no surprise. "With God all things are possible." But when a human being undertakes that same project, what then? Nietzsche is about to change the course of nature, rather like making water run up hill. "I have the destiny of all water in my hand." He sought to transform human nature, beginning with his own; "I have wrung from these years much in the way of purification and burnishing of the soul." What, accordingly, I do not understand is how a mere human being should not only have dreamed up such a task but how he could over some years have worked with energy and passion to perform it. But to understand this is to understand "the Inexorable Tyrant" and "his ways are past finding out." We who dilly-dally through life and are not the chosen servants of the Most High can only stand and gape. How is it possible? With the Inexorable Tyrant all things are possible.

There are varieties of divine madness.

Nietzsche wrote of Socrates, "Socrates was the buffoon who made others take him seriously," and he wrote of the "Socratic wisdom full of pranks" and of "the assurance of the great ironist." Here is a suggestion as to how one should read Nietzsche. Nietzsche, too, is a buffoon, a prankster, as assured as Socrates. As man did not discover that Socrates was a buffoon but took him seriously, so too man would not discover that Nietzsche was a buffoon but would take him seriously. After two thousand years someone would come along and say, "But Nietzsche was a buffoon. He was only fooling." Naturally the pranks did not show. The idea is intriguing. During all those years there was an understanding between Nietzsche and God that Nietzsche was to do that. And the object? "To purify and burnish men's souls," to resist the evil one. I forgot something! Socrates was most of all the buffoon when he said, "God orders me to fulfill the philosopher's mission of searching into myself and other men." In a similar fashion Nietzsche would have been most of all the buffoon when he said, "The tyrant, the Inexorable Tyrant, wills that." When a buffoon says what is true, it is still buffoonery. Imagine it, making a career of one lifelong prank!

Nietzsche said that he held the destiny of mankind in his hand. Is there anyone else of whom one might say this or who said this of himself? I am not going to mention Hitler. There, I did not. But there is someone who might have said this, did not say it, and if he did hold the destiny of mankind in his hand did not know it. There was at the time that Nietzsche lived a man who was handy with tools, and he made an automobile. He held something in his hand. I will not say that he transformed human nature, but he did transform a lot or was instrumental in transforming a lot. I do not think Nietzsche was handy with tools, at least, nothing has been made of it. What then were his instruments? At any rate, Nietzsche, it seems, was neither the first nor the last to have had his hands full. What that man with tools did we have seen done. That was possible.

Who is this Nietzsche? He is the earthshaker, the cloud-gatherer, the hurler of the thunderbolt, lord of counsel, lord of the storm-cloud, most dread son of Chronos, lord of the lightning, aegis-bearer, king among gods and men.

Again, as in the case of the writer of the *Notes from Underground*, one must ask, Why did he write these things? This will be especially so with those readers who cannot conceive that a man should have tried to do what Nietzsche said he was trying to do. So let us ask, Why? Here then is an unlikely suggestion. Early Nietzsche discovered that opinions he expressed were shocking. Like Ivan, he may have held these opinions. Once, however, he discovered that the opinion was shocking, this added spice to the expression of that opinion. It gave him a sense of power, something which he also had a taste for. This, expression of shocking opinions—shocking people, began to have a special attraction for him. So he began making up and cultivating shocking opinions. And the game took on the character of, Do I dare? and with each more shocking opinion a new test of his daring arose. He would say not, "Do I dare to eat a peach?" but, "Do I dare to say this?" He realizes that with the enjoyment of the effect of his expressed opinion there would be a price. There would be alienation, hostility, loneliness. He seems to have realized this. He calculated the cost. But since he was the author not only of the opinion, but of the shock and of the alienation, with every new shock and the new alienation, he found new witness of his power, of his freedom, of his independence. That such freedom, such independence, comes dear he knew to begin with. In this way his life continued to be a testing of his will to shock, to alienate, to be free. But since he has to keep up the tension, he had to devise not merely new shockers, but shockers more shocking than the shockers that went before. I am not sure that his expressed opinions, shockers on this view, can be arranged to show this progression in shock and in the intensity of the enjoyment of what a daring young man can do without a trapeze. Would a man, someone may ask, give up so much, the price of accelerated shock, in order to revel in the upset people one has upset? "Is not this the great Babylon I have built?" Is not this the great shock I shocked them with? I am certainly not suggesting that Nietzsche told those he shocked that he said what he said to shock them. Had he done that he would have been deprived of the spectacle of his own power—which he had the will to.

Am I serious? No, no, not altogether. It is, at any rate, possible that when he shocked and angered people he enjoyed the sense of his having done that. And why should not a man develop a taste for that? And have we not all learned from Nietzsche that we are all, insofar as we have any initiative, greedy and joyous in the lust for life which is power? Everyone has his specialty. Some men dominate, control—how? By shock. One can appreciate that a man to be powerful in that way, must know how to shock, must know in what areas men are most susceptible, and then he must have a gift for saying what is shocking. It is very much like sharing omnipotence, or, at least, a piece of it. One can imagine

Nietzsche saying something and watching his friends squirm, and then not only friends and acquaintances; and by and by whole cities, etc., illusion supplying more and more. Nietzsche, our high-voltage man, the man out of whom one may still get a charge, out of which, our charge, he gets a charge. Did he shock people? Of course. And was he surprised? No. Nietzsche, the foremost shocker, a greater than Voltaire, was not surprised.

Lengthier *Zettel*

These fragments I have shored against
my ruin(s)

T. S. Eliot, *The Waste Land*

I

This paper was written for and read at a symposium at the College of Wooster, Wooster, Ohio in October of 1976. The German word *Zettel* means scrap, or slip of paper. The executors of Ludwig Wittgenstein's literary estate found a collection of philosophical fragments on slips of paper in a box and published this collection under the title *Zettel*. Bouwsma borrowed the title and qualified it as lengthier *Zettel* because the fragments that he assembled here, though somewhat longer than Wittgenstein's, were like his in treating the subject matter piecemeal.

To inspire with concern and unrest. "The maximum of what one human being can do for another . . . is to inspire him with concern and unrest." That should provide us with a hint concerning the subjective thinker. The question is as to how he does that. He cannot do this by saying "Boo!" or pulling faces, or wearing a Halloween mask. We must ask more about this concern and unrest. We may be sure that it is concern about one's life, what sort of man he is and is to become. This writer is a disturber of a man's peace—or his sleep, as Nietzsche would say, "Sleepers, awake!"

2

Is belief in God rational?

Is belief in God rational?
Is love of God rational?
Is worship rational?
Is praising God rational?
Is singing rational?

Is this the way to express the issue that concerned K.[Kierkegaard]? Try it. So some people said, Yes, it is rational. Others said, No, it is irrational. And what does K. say? I do not know that K. asks this question. I think the response to this should be that this language does not apply. One might as sensibly ask, Is

God rational? And that means what? Is he still able to take care of his business? In case of an accident a man may be rendered unconscious, but he may also be delirious and be irrational, speaking of things of long ago as though they were present. Has God had an accident?

Does Freud in effect say that belief in God, whether Jewish or Christian, is irrational? Another imaginative realization of mind or wish? And what then is rational? Having a human father and going to him for help, saying, for instance, "Dad, can I have the car tonight?"

3

The offer. The offer is there on the page. The words are there. They are presented as spoken by a man. Why indeed should not these words be spoken by a man? They are, after all, words, only words. But you do not realize what words these are and what the offer is. Have you ever heard of eternal life, and now of the offer of eternal life, ever heard of such a thing? You and the rest of us, ever since Socrates helped to make up one of the favorite syllogisms, Barbara, have known that man is mortal, every one of them, except for Enoch and Elijah. And here in this book you can read of a man, a man, mind you, who offers eternal life, and not to one or two only, to a few favorites, but to anyone who will accept it. Did you get that? You still do not believe it? Let me add something to this. Not only is the story the story, for it is a story, of a man who makes an offer, but also of people, of other men and women who accept the offer. Eternal life, in a way, who wouldn't go for that? And yet it does seem foolish, a man offering people eternal life when anyone can see that the man who offers it is mortal like the rest of us and likely to die quite young himself. And yet there it is, a man passing out, not to customers, but to anyone, a gift. This is a gift. There is nothing to pay, nothing to earn. One might well suppose that someone made up the story, a crazy story, for who, what man, in his right mind would make such an offer ("Come and get it") and who, otherwise in his right mind, would come forward to accept such a gift. One would certainly expect that those interested would first examine what was offered, much as men do a gift horse, though in this case it would most likely be the man who was making the offer whom those interested would examine, not that that would help much. For how would a man who made such an offer ever assure any who came forward that he could provide what he offered?

Has there ever been anything like this in the history of the world?

Perhaps something like it. At least one can imagine something like it. One can imagine one of the richest men in the world one day, glad about something, making an announcement in the newspapers that he will on the next day give away a lot of money, let us say, in front of his hotel. One might describe this as an offer. Everyone is invited. No one knows whether he has the money he says he will give away. Of course, nearly everyone would like some of that money. People read the newspaper. The next day arrives. The rich man walks out of the hotel at dawn in the morning, expecting to give away money. There is no one to meet him. A few people pass by and glance at him and smile. Some laugh. The idea of a man giving away money to anyone and without asking any questions, and without signatures, and without a name of his own, anonymous money, has struck most people as absurd. The money is suspect. It must be counterfeit and if not counterfeit, just pennies. And who in 1976 is going to get up early or late to receive a gift of a piece of paper or a penny? Some people are angry. They think the man should be jailed or driven out of town. It is a hoax. In any case, the rich man has unwittingly placed himself in danger. Surely an investigation should be made. Who is this man? Clearly it is not safe to give away money so freely.

Eternal life is not money. It does not come in denominations of coins and bills. Still, I remember now the phrase "Buy without money and without price." Money too may be bought. And in this case money, too, is offered without money and without price, not bought.

What did I want this for?

4

What is eternal life? It is a form of engagement, a struggle, a striving. It involves a future in which the end of one's striving is fulfilled. And so what is offered in the offer of eternal life? A new start. A task. A venture. A never-ending river of turns and windings with new obstacles and new overcomings. Is that the way to speak of eternal life? Eternal life has a beginning but no end. "I began eternal life a year ago." It is something like a career. "I began my career (I am a doctor) last May." A career may go on for 40 years. That too involves a task. The task is open to public view. The doctor has many patients. He keeps up with the newest. He is successful. But eternal life goes on in the stillness. There is no public and no office. And there are no yearly reports. "How are you doing?"

5

Is K.'s polemic obsolete? I have said earlier that the polemic against the Hegelians is now obsolete since there aren't any Hegelians any more. They are few, only fossil Hegelians. And now I have been reminded that the polemic against the great uncloud of witnesses who said, "We are Christians," being under the illusion that they were Christians, is also obsolete. For there are not many of those any more either. These days there is no advantage in being a Christian. Little prestige attaches to this. So if we or if anyone were to wage a kind of warfare, such as K. waged, the Hegelians and "I am a Christian" having passed away, against whom should one go out to fight? There is always oneself, of course, but one would prefer to fight a whole army. Is there someone? Is there such an army? Isn't K. obsolete?

6

K. and our forgetting. In a passage above I introduced the question whether K. was doing the sort of thing W.[Wittgenstein] was doing. I went on to describe something that K. was doing. He said he was setting forth the ethical. I went on to say that the situation required this since men had forgotten what it means to be a man, and so on. I wrote in this connection of two concerns, concerns which may compete within the same person or between different persons or different groups of persons. "So you are a Nobel prize winner and you have not read *Hamlet* since you were in high school nor ever heard of Tolstoy's *23 Tales?*" So you make such beautiful lace, the lace of Lilla, and have never asked yourself, And who or what will make beautiful lace of me? This following is a sentence from K. which I may have misunderstood: "My principal thought was that in our age because of the great increase in knowledge, we had forgotten what it means to exist (and not just to know) and what inwardness signified and that the misunderstanding between speculative philosophy and Christianity was explicable on that basis" (*Postscript*, p. 223). K. describes this as "my principal thought." In case someone has forgotten something, the thing to do in case it matters, is to remind him, "Say, you forgot something. Let me tell you." But it isn't that simple. It is not a piece of information or a whole book or many memories that one has forgotten and that K. would bring to mind. The kind of forgetting K. has in mind is more like atrophy. Once you could read poetry, it was one of your delights, and now all you can think of are the huge turtles around the Galapagos and what they eat, and do they make a noise like a fish if a fish makes a noise? Have I got this straight? Isn't K.'s task more like that of re-educating the explorer of Galapagos? Perhaps it is too late for that, and besides who said he wanted to be re-educated? Still, in case something has been forgotten, the remedy is surely the reminder. Perhaps this forgetting is more like neglect, like neglecting exercise, taking a walk. And so what one has forgotten is not something one once knew but some things one perhaps used to do or used to think about. According to this understanding of K. written here, K.'s task is to help to prevent such forgetting by supplying reminders. The reminders, however, are not to take the form of blunt counsels. One is not to tell one to do something. "Think on these things." The idea is to awaken in one the desire to do what comes naturally. The question or the problem is, how are you to get a man who thinks about turtles, who never tires thinking about turtles, taking their measurements, 24, 36, 36, and studying their toes, etc., one day to think and to consider what sort of creature *he* is. If the question is put to him, as you, together with him, admire turtles, "And what are we doing under the sun?" he may say, "We are admiring turtles." And that may be a beginning. Is man more than a turtle? ("The voice of the turtle is heard in the land"—a different turtle.)

Obviously I need some help in connection with the thought "We had forgotten what it means to exist and what inwardness signifies." Just what have we forgotten? Here are some questions: "How did that happen? How could one forget something as important as that? Presumably it is important. *Is it rather like forgetting to eat?*" There are other questions. If someone should get to worry about this, is there something he can do? K. seems to think that we who have forgotten are not aware we have forgotten anything. "We haven't forgotten anything. Nothing is missing in our lives. We have simply outgrown our childhood. It often happens to children." I just asked above, "Is it like forgetting to eat?" but perhaps this is a more suitable analogy: "Haven't you forgotten to see to your proteins?" ("A one-sided diet.") If, of course, we say that we haven't forgotten anything, then it won't do to tell him what he has forgotten. He will not recognize what he is told as anything he has forgotten or cares to remember. Hence he has first to be brought to the point where he begins to miss what he has forgotten. That is one of K.'s worries. This sounds a little like Socrates. "You have forgotten something." Socrates spent a good part of his life trying to remember. And it was terribly important to him. He went about this in a curious way, looking for what he forgot in other people's memories. K., presumably, knows what it is we have forgotten.

I have already suggested that we are not simple, not that this is news. It is out of an aspect of this complexity that a part of K.'s polemic is to be understood. Man is greedy for knowledge. Men want to know. In 1976 it is sometimes said that man already knows too much. Man can control a gun with a finger, a finger he cannot control. He isn't big enough for what he knows. Men used to say this not of what he knows but of his breeches, too big for his breeches. But there is also the ethical, an interest and a concern older than this interest in knowing. It is this conflict for dominance, the dominance of this interest in knowledge that has made manikins of man. As we know, K. uses the words "objective" and "subjective" to describe the contrast. The idea is that the subjective, too, requires attention and nurture. "Why have a few become immortal as enthusiastic lovers, a few as high-minded lovers . . . ?" Real lovers are very rare. "(Why) a select circle of devout men and women?" It must be clear that K., in passages such as these, is lamenting neglect. And for what? The worms in the library, the worms in the books, who might have been Romeos or Horatios or saints. Those worms have said, "It is better to know."

Concerning this reading of something in K. it is clear that W. has no part in this. ("If a lacemaker were to produce ever so beautiful laces, it nevertheless makes one sad to contemplate such a poor stunted creature . . . and it is impossible to admire the laces without shedding tears for the lacemaker.")[1]

7

The hidden inwardness. The hidden inwardness, what is that? What could it be but a man's resolve, his decision. "I will follow." "I am a pilgrim." "This one thing I do." "I will be faithful." "I have made my vows." All this goes on unseen. No one may know that any such vow has been made. It is a matter between a man and his maker. It is this, the decision, the venture, that K. means by action. And this must now be realized, the vow kept. "I have made a covenant." This idea or this

---

1. Søren Kierkegaard, *Concluding Unscientific Postscript,* trans. David Swensen (Princeton, N.J.: Princeton University Press, 1941), p. 268.

explication of inwardness may relieve us of a lot of puzzlement. It seems now like a beam of light through the haze.

8

The paradox. K. has a use for such phrases as "the essentially comprehensible" and "the essentially incomprehensible" and more startling: "Believing against the understanding," and "Faith's crucifixion of the understanding." These expressions come into play in K.'s thinking about the Paradox, "the babe in the manger." What child is this? Here is a sentence: "But that the eternal should come . . . , is born, grows up, and dies—is a breach with all thinking." There are other expressions, such as "cannot be thought." These are K.'s expositions of: "to the Greeks foolishness." We are all Greeks.

The paradox. I said that there must be a Scriptural equivalent of this. And this occurred to me: None exist. But one may find some clues to this. Consider these two expressions in the Scriptures: "Thou are the Christ, the Son of God," and "My Lord and my God!" I need not, I think, remind you of the circumstances under which these words are spoken. They are spoken in the presence of and—to a man. If now we ask, What do these sentences mean? we may understand that question, following W., to be the same as, How are those sentences used? The answer may be, Those sentences are the expressions of faith and of commitment. "It is an awful thing." K. is fond of the word "passion." This takes place between one man and another. It is a form of surrender. Now if someone, also present, were to say, "How can that be? This man is a man.—and God is God.—No man can be God and God cannot be man." And he would shake his head over this. And K., who is also present in a sense, spanning the centuries, says, "Stop! It is a paradox." And this is a way of saying, Those sentences cannot be understood by taking those sentences apart and then seeing that they cannot be understood by putting those words together again. Those sentences are not intended to describe anything as though those who speak them, with their seeing eyes, had discovered the divine hidden in this man visible to all men. They are not seeing the invisible clothed in this otherwise man like us. Those who say that in making these declarations these men are projecting their longings, their wishes, might be considered nearer the truth than are those who say that they are talking nonsense. When, accordingly, K. says, "Keep off! Stop! It is a paradox," this is his way of saying, "A confession, a declaration, is not a piece of information. This is holy ground. Remove your clumsy shoes."

9

Socrates. Perhaps we can understand Socrates as a man who thinks of himself as a subject, as a servant, but he does not know what or whom he serves nor how. This is his ignorance. We might say that he knows that he should be virtuous but he does not know what virtue is. Now I am for once clear about Socrates's ignorance. This would, of course, not have bothered him except that he still has the burden of his being a servant, a servant from the beginning. It is as though he knew there must be a Moses or other prophets who would know what he does not know. Was Socrates distressed about this, worried? He did not show it. Socrates is a little like those who expect a Messiah—who does not come. He, the Messiah, will come later. He will. There is risk.

I remember at other times worrying about what to make of the idea of Socrates as a subjective thinker. I had in mind in those days the idea that Socrates never told anyone anything but that he always aimed at getting those he talked to to think for themselves. He never had any results. He stirred things up, kept things moving. This obviously had something to do with what he regarded as his task. And that now seemed to be to hold people responsible for what they were saying at the same time that he pressed them to say something. But following Craft's idea, what makes Socrates a subjective thinker has to do with how he regarded what he was doing and why he did it. He did it because he was commanded to do it. He was under orders. The important thing is not what the task is but that a man should have a task, a task laid upon him.

What an idea! That a man should have a task, and that he has come to it and that it should not end. The task is never finished. Hand to the plough. A furrow into the horizon.

10

The Hegelians and the passion for knowledge. The Hegelians were metaphysicians. The universe, reality, has beginning, middle, and end, and they got the grandstand grand view, from nothing at all through Becoming, a stirring in the old rags, to all's quiet on the thinking front, reality in its Sunday clothes. You might say that such a view is a remarkable achievement, something on the order of the Eiffel Tower, or another tower of sorts too, made however not of beams of steel but of ideas, harder and more durable, immoveable like the conclusion of a syllogism. It must have been a delight and the pride of this thinker. "I will build you a tower," and then he would put words together and call it truth. I do not suppose that K. objected to this. He may have appreciated architecture as he did Tivoli. (That doesn't sound like a Danish word.) That is not where the trouble lay.

The trouble lay in that those who had such a grand view regarded the Scriptures—I am avoiding the word "Christianity"—as presenting a more or less competing, but not so complete and grand, view of Reality. So we get the idea of metaphysics No. 1, being superseded by metaphysics No. 2. It is as though there were people who in an unadvantageous position had a view of the Grand Canyon and then others came along who stood closer to the rim and looked and saw more. They said, "We have seen and saw what you see, but we see much more, and how glorious the view is!" Many of them came over to the edge of the rim, and they said, "You are right."

I am sure that this misconception is common. Liberal theology.

It won't make any difference that the misconception referred to arises out of the fact that we know so much. If we know so much and that is the source of our trouble, the remedy would seem to be, See to it that we get to know less. Too late for that. And so we must find another way. Of course, the Scriptures are not another book in metaphysics. How to show that? The grammar of metaphysics versus the grammar of the Scriptures.

I got this slightly wrong. It isn't that we know so much, though that has something to do with it. It is that what we have, in having knowledge, makes knowledge so precious to us, and makes us so greedy for it, that we make of knowing the end-all of our lives. What else could there be? No doubt in our own time, when we are all educated, and Knowledge, or what passes for Knowledge, is rampant among us, and we hear that Knowledge is the good or the road to happiness, no wonder that we heap up knowledge more and more. There was once a miser, so they said, who was very rich. He had so much gold. He loved his gold and desired more gold. He once said that he wished that everything might be changed into gold. And his wish was granted! That is a little like the way in which K. would have us think about ourselves. We have had such a passion for knowledge that we, too, in a sense have wished that everything should be changed into knowledge. In our case, too, the wish has been granted. And we are stunned. (I remember now that the wish was everything we read should be changed into knowledge. And it, too, was so. In that way we have been deprived.)

This was King Midas. I think it well to add that after he entreated Dionysus to give him relief, he was ordered to wash himself in a river. And what is a man in our time to do when everything he reads turns to knowledge? It is not, of course, that he complains of this. A man may be sick and have rosy cheeks.

I I

My task. My task—well, what is it? When the young man asked: What must I do to inherit eternal life? there was a reply. I do not suppose that the task was to seek eternal life. Is that perhaps the incentive for undertaking the task? Jesus then assigned to the man the task, Keep the commandments. "That have I done from my youth." "What then do I yet lack?" When Jesus told him to sell all his goods, etc., was that in effect to tell him he had not kept the law? It is very difficult to keep this law, and keeping this law is keeping oneself. "Follow me" is to follow along a way that is rough. For one must be rough on oneself. What, then, is the task? It is "to keep oneself unspotted from the world." The leopard and his spots. "Out damned spot"—for everyone.

A man who loves money and, wanting to be rich, gets to know the prices of everything and knows when to buy and when to sell. He has taken upon himself and may succeed—in the world. But here is a different task. "Fast from evil." "Depart from evil and do good." "Love me, and if ye love me you will keep my commandments." This man has made a vow and the task of his life is to keep that vow. "The pledge of allegiance." It is like a marriage vow, for richer for poorer, "in sickness and in health, until death do us part." Loyalty, In thought, word, and deed. "Thou good and faithful servant." A servant.

When K. uses this language intending to make the language new and fresh, he also risks concealing the meaning. Then one has to use the language one did not understand in the first place to understand the language designed to help one understand the language one did not understand in the first place.

I 2

Privacy. Craft said, You can never know whether or not someone has made a vow, whether he has said, "Yes," and meant it. But, of course, you may trust that someone has. So if I say, "So-and-so is one of them," that will show something about me. The vow is made in secret. I may stand in awe of him. My attitude towards him is a revelation of my trust. Only God knows that I am or am not deceived. The man I trust may put on the shows and trappings of the devout man. Where are vows made, "in the heart or in the head"? If a man says, "I have made a vow," does that show he has? I think that K. says about the Christian that he knows about himself what he must do and what he does when he does it. But he cannot tell his brother. I guess we must ask, Why should he? Still the question arises: How then is a man "to confess me before men"? What is "confessing"? If a man makes a vow and serves, he is not to hide his light under a bushel. "Let your light shine before men." I guess it isn't that what a man says or does, then, gives anyone information, but it may serve to make another pause and wonder. "Where have you been?" "Sweet bells jangled out of tune, jangled again into tune." The gospels tell us of people who followed him and gave their lives—so there could be such people. But the Bible tells us secrets that we could otherwise not know. After that we must take human beings on trust—not that we can trust a man if he says, "I did," but there is more than that to a man. Part of the trouble is that even if the man did do something, what he did may not be clear even to himself, and even if it is clear, it may not be what is required.

A Lengthy *Zettel*

"A Lengthy *Zettel*" was written in January of 1978 and, as far as is known, is the last paper Bouwsma wrote.

If a Jew were writing about God, his God, that is, there is no God in general, whom would he mention? Naturally he would mention Abraham, Isaac, and Jacob, and perhaps, Moses. There are many names. He might even mention Jesus Christ. That name would come in for honorable mention. He was a distinguished rabbi. And if Harun El Raschid or Assad Kadat were writing about God, his God, there is no God in general, whom would he mention? Naturally, he would mention Mohammed, no, not Mohammed Ali, but the Muphta Mohammed, the Muphta, his God's prophet. And if a Christian were writing about God, his God, there is no God in general, a believer writing about believing that or in his God, whom would he mention? Well, he might mention Abraham, Isaac, and Jacob, and he might mention King David and Isaiah. Anyone else, any other name, "a name far above every name"? "And his name shall be called." You would not expect a Christian, writing about his God, not to mention this name. And who then or what name would that be? It may be that to mention that name would be to admit to a certain holy foolishness, especially, foolishness. That would be embarrassing. What name is that? I forgot.

And what if a man were to write about God in general? I have been saying that there is no

God in general, but devotees of the God in general do write about the God in general. And who or what name would this writer mention in writing of the God in general? I have not said "his" God since God in general is an idea and no God. This God doesn't do anything and isn't supposed to. And so what name does this writer mention? Not Abraham, not Isaac, not Jacob, not Mohammed, neither Muphta nor Ali, nor that other name said by another writer to be greater than any name. In fact this writer would exclude any foolishness. As far as I can make out he won't mention any name at all, not even the name of man in general, were there such a name. And what was that name greater than any name? I'm sorry. I forgot.

It seems obvious now that there are at least three Gods. And should I add the God in general? The God in general is surprisingly popular, especially for a god who never does anything. Even people who are not devotees love to write about him or it, presumably under the illusion they are writing about one of the three mentioned above. If someone were to say, "Oh, you are writing about the god in general," the writer might be shocked that anyone should think that. But then if one were to go on to say, "How is it that you, a Jew, should write all that and not mention Abraham, Isaac, and Jacob and not refer to your subject as the God of Abraham, Isaac, and Jacob," he might respond, flustered, "Oh, I forgot." That would be an odd thing to forget. And was it not the brother of Harun El Raschid who wrote a long piece about God and who did not mention Mecca or the mountain or Mohammed who was the God's prophet? That writer, when reproached by one of his readers, did he not say, "I forgot"? An odd thing to forget. Even I, who am not a Muslim, would know that the name of Mohammed should have been mentioned. How should we have known Allah save through his prophet?

I do not suppose that any Christian writer, writing blind as it were, writing about God and believing and about how blessed and crazy it is, would fail to mention that name I referred to above. There is a good reason for this. For in the case of the Jew these names he might have mentioned were only the names of servants. "Go from your country . . . to the land, that I will show you." In the case of Harun El Raschid the name he might especially have mentioned was only the name of a prophet. Mohammed was not Allah. But in the case of the Christian writer, the name he would not have mentioned would not have been the name of a man who was told to go nor the name of a prophet. What name was that? Again, I forgot. In any case were there such a writer who wrote and who perhaps thought about his God, his indeed, though he could not think of his God's name, and never mentioned his name in what he wrote, some readers might not understand him. Some would say, "Oh, he is writing about the God in general, not the God of Abraham, Isaac, and Jacob, not the God of Mohammed, nor any other." He might be alarmed at this. He would say, "Why, I was thinking of him and his name with every word I wrote." "But why, then, did you not mention his name?" And to that he would reply, "How could I in the company I keep? They would laugh at me." I am, of course, just imagining someone who has all the right thoughts, but is not very good at names. Without names it is difficult to distinguish one God from another. How many Gods are there? Four? (Without a scorecard you won't know the players.)

First I squared the circle.
Then I wrestled with a unicorn.
At another time I invented perpetual motion.
On a Tuesday I proved the existence of God.
Later I pulled a rabbit out of a hat with no rabbit in it.
After that I circled the square on my tricycle.
They say I am a genius.
Which God was that? The one you proved the existence of.

If anyone believes all or some of these things in the Apostles' Creed, he must have won all the prizes in mathematics. He must be very good at reasoning, syllogisms, and calculation. He must be smart, eerie-rational. He is, perhaps, quick as lightning. He read it or he heard it, he thought, he understood, one, two, three, and he believed. Then he pushed the button and rested.

"Can a man by thinking add a cubit to this stature?" Why, yes, he can if he is a philosopher. "And can a man by thinking find out God?" Why, yes, if he is a philosopher. And which God would that be? The God one can find out by thinking. That is the God of the philosopher. If Abraham had been a philosopher he wouldn't have had to wait until God found him. He would then have sat down on a stone and thought and so found out God. What is a man rational for save that by thinking he should do things? What things? Things such as adding a cubit to his stature and, of course, finding out God. Many philosophers have done these things and do. Some try and do not quite make it. Had Abraham continued to sit on that stone he never would have left Ur of Chaldees, quite a nice place to bring up a family. As it is he left under orders, leaving the stone behind, the philosophers' stone.

Appendix

The two short pieces that follow pose special problems for the reader. They were written to play a role in some particular discussion or colloquy and thereby presuppose a context that the reader is not given. Accordingly, they are not appropriate for the body of this volume. However, they reflect Bouwsma's manner of doing philosophy, and there is much that can be gathered from these observations, including suggestions about myth, pictures, and reading Scripture. Internal evidence suggests 1963 as the date for "Myth and the Language of Scriptures" and 1966 for "The Biblical Picture of Human Life."

MYTH AND THE LANGUAGE OF SCRIPTURE

Such expressions as *"the Sacred Scriptures," "the Holy Scriptures,"* perhaps "the word of God," "the divine word," are not in the ordinary sense descriptive. They are not like "There are thirty-nine books in the Old Testament." They might be described as expressing attitudes of believers to the Scriptures, and they serve to instill such attitudes in others. The use of the halo in paintings of our Lord and of the saints.

The dean of Saint Paul's says that the account of the ascension is a myth. He meant no harm, but when the question was put to him as to what else was myth and what was not—in the Scriptures, that is—he said that the meaning of the word "myth" would have to be considered. This does, indeed, require explanation. To say that that account is a myth is, no doubt, to say that in a way it is false—that is, when read and understood in a certain way—and that in a way it is true—that is when read and understood in a certain other way. One must read this account in the way in which other myths are read. But what myths then would the dean propose to us as examples? Most of us do not read myths, and if we do, they are read as fantastic old Greek stories. Freud did something in the interest of reading myths, teaching us how to read them—in a certain way. This, at any rate, is intelligible. A myth is a chest and Freud gives us a key to unlock it, to steal, perhaps, treasure. Does the dean have a key? Where, by the way, did Freud get his key? Perhaps there are a number of keys. And how to begin with does one recognize the myth as a myth? Is it by the fantastic element? I suppose one recognizes a myth before one asks, Now what is the meaning? I know. We all know that there are myths. Dead religions are replete with myths. That is their literature: So if you want to know what a myth is I can read you a dozen. There are books and books of myths. They make good children's stories. Are fairy-tales to be read too as myths? So I give you samples of myths. But if you ask me what the myth means I may not know. A myth, I take it, has a meaning. A myth is like an allegory. The characters and the events involved are symbolic. Now then to read a myth one must understand the symbolism. Does one discover that so-and-so is a myth? Did the dean always say that this is a myth, or did he just lately come to say this? Is reading this account as a myth just one way of reading it and does one suddenly pass from one way of reading it to another? For centuries this account, this passage, in Scripture has been read in one way—so it can be read in that way—and does the dean now say that that is the wrong way? Is it that the dean found out a lot of things and this made him change his way of reading this? I don't suppose he has found out anything. But things have changed. Attitudes towards belief. Science. "Man cannot live by—."

This particular passage in Scripture is not isolated. It isn't like the story of Jonah and the whale. Someone's saying that this is a myth is not tied in with other stories, isn't a part of a larger story. But the story of the ascension is tied to the account of the resurrection and the events which occurred between the day of the resurrection and the ascension. How far then is the dean to go? "Demythologizing"—that, I suppose, means removing the myths. I suppose the idea is that we no longer need myths, we no longer need the resurrection and the ascension. Something more nebulous will do.

(Jonah and the whale. Red Riding Hood's grandmother and the wolf.) In Catholic literature legends play a great role. Relics, images.

Religious language—psalms, songs, exhortations, proclamations, proverbs, lamentations, prophecies, sacred history ("what God hath done").

But I don't suppose this is what will be discussed. There are philosophical problems. And what are they? The distinction between religious belief and other beliefs and knowledge, etc.

Religious language. Examples of it. "I am the Lord, thy God. . . ." and the 23rd Psalm and Psalm 51 and passages in Isaiah, stories of the nativity, the Sermon on the Mount, and the chapters 14–17 in the gospel of Saint John, etc.

What's the problem? Here it is, a book of religious language. You've been reading it all your life—now what do you want? Confusion. You may read it as secular history, or as poetry or literature, as philosophy—in which case all that is religiously essential is philosophically accidental—hence not only dispensable but a nuisance.

Teaching people how to read the Scriptures.—Kierkegaard.

Religious language. The language God speaks. "And the Lord said. . . ." And the language of those who understand Him. The language of a certain communication. A conversation. Sometimes "God" introduces himself.

"In the beginning God created . . . ," not "I" created.

Here is another approach.

In religious, Scriptural language, there are certain words which commonly give people trouble. There are the words "God" (I am the Lord, thy God"), "truth" ("I am the truth"), and "spirit" (God is a spirit). And there is the word "love." There are these other words: "sin," "guilt," "forgiveness," "repentance," "justification," "sanctification," "eternal life," "the kingdom of heaven," and so on.

In connection with all these expressions the question arises, "What is—?" And this question may be asked either by someone who is well acquainted with the Scriptures and what he needs is reminders—there may be some question as to how he comes to ask—whatever it is he asks—or by someone to whom this language is strange and he needs an explanation. The idea of reminders is, I guess, simple enough. This may, however, be fairly extensive, depending upon what gives rise to the question. Sometimes one may be asking: How does Saint Paul use the expression "justification"? And this may require one's review of connections of the use of this word with that of other words. The whole perspective must be provided. The explanation must be given as a means of helping people to read. In this sense the apostle Philip helped the Ethiopian eunuch to read.

There are other sorts of questions. There are obviously philosophical ones such as, How can a perfectly good and all-powerful God permit one child to die? This is usually stated—I mean the difficulty—in terms of holocausts, disasters, famine, war, etc. How can God—? Also: How can God who is just, forgive—forgive everything? (The reconciliation of justice and mercy.) Perhaps there are ever so many other philosophical problems. *How can God create something out of nothing? How was or is the Incarnation possible?* (How is it possible that God should be nailed to a cross?) How is the resurrection possible? How is miracle possible? These are the typical philosophical problems. And the difficulties are rooted in the language. Is that right? This is complicated, for though the difficulties are rooted in language—there is usually animus. This, however, may be no more than the normal orneriness of a disputant.

The problems involved here are troublesome to all bright people. And it is well to get as clear about them as we can. The troubles arise in this way: A good part of the language of the Scriptures, the words, phrases, and some of the connections, are the same as those of nonscriptural language. And in general the uses of these expressions overlap. But in a great number of cases there are deviations. It is these deviations which come into the open in these cases. It is easy to see this. God is our heavenly father, "Our Father which art in heaven." This is figurative language and we understand it only by way of our understanding the meaning of the word "father" in our daily and normal family lives, and in connection with this the attitudes of children, their trust and dependence, etc. "As a father pitieth his children, so the Lord pitieth them. . . ." This is the language which is intended to bring his pity to those who suffer, his comfort to the sorrowing, etc. This is a constant theme, e.g., "I am the Good Shepherd" and "the Good Samaritan". I was about to suggest that there are variations in the appeals according to our various states. For those who need help and comfort he is the good and merciful. For those who are hard and unrepentant, he is a just and "sure avenger of all who are oppressed." *God is all things to all men according to their need of him in the pathway of regeneration.* His wrath is also required. God's cunning. One can see immediately how tempting this parallelism in the language is—"As a father pitieth his children," "As a father chasteneth," "As a father careth for"—"How much more will he care for you . . . ?" God makes distinctions, all right. But not "As a father giveth his children toothache"—No father would do that; at least, no father who would be respected.

One must always ask in connection with any passage in Scripture, To whom is this addressed?

There are philosophical difficulties also called contradictions. The language gives rise to them as language does otherwise. "How can . . . ?"

There is something else. But I scarcely know how to describe it, whether as an ordinary misunderstanding or as a confusion. Suppose someone says, "Shut the door," and the servant now instead of shutting the door, once a week makes a fuss, gets dressed in his best clothes, and sings and kneels and bows himself and repeats aloud, "Shut the door," "Shut the door," but it never occurs to him to shut the door. What would you call that? Or consider this: A man is left a legacy and he is told to spend it. But the man never bothers to claim his legacy and, of course, never spends any of it. And yet he thinks he enjoys his legacy. To something like this K. [Kierkegaard] addressed himself in *Fear and Trembling.* What is faith?

There were, as I read K., especially two things that he fought. One was the philosophers who "improved" upon Christianity with what one might describe as a higher view, a superior insight; and the other was the theologians who reduced Christianity to a form of right (or wrong) doctrine. Both are forms of intellectualism. In both cases it was not ignorance of the Word, the Scriptures, which was responsible, but misunderstanding. Is "misunderstanding" the right word? If I say, "Shut the door," and you say, "Absolutely," not a doubt about it, and you go on counting your loose change or chuck Annabelle under the chin, what would you call that? Misunderstanding?

If I bring you good news—enough to change your life—and now nothing happens, and yet you show no signs at all of your not understanding me, what then?

At any rate, *Fear and Trembling* is an attempt on K.'s part to introduce his readers to the concept of faith. Obviously two things are involved. What he does first is to present for our recollection the hero of faith on the occasion, the one great occasion which exemplifies what I may call the workings of faith. And after having done that, he guards against misunderstanding by presenting other heroes, knights, not of faith, but of resignation and of other forms of human response to the trials of life, which are in some ways similar to those of the hero of faith. And these are not definitions. These are cases. How does one sharpen distinctions? By presenting cases—in many respects similar—and then making the differences stand out. Subtle distinctions. As I recollect it, this is the method K. pursues in the study of faith. Look, look! At Abraham, the hero of faith! Now look at these heroes, also heroes, but not heroes of faith.

No man but one of broad culture and wide reading could have written such a book. But why should he have written such a book? What need was there? Apparently, the people for whom K. was writing no longer knew what faith was. So he wrote this book to remind them. And yet it isn't that they did not know the story of Abraham. They had heard it a thousand times. There are two ways in which they might have lost the point. They might have read the story or heard it without close attention. They could not have distinguished between the story of Abraham and the story of Agamemnon, who sacrificed a daughter, or between Abraham and Jephthah, who also sacrificed a daughter. That is strictly a matter of quick intelligence. Heroes of faith and heroes of resignation! They, these people, might themselves not have gotten mixed up in this. They might also have been percipient in the reading of other literature, travel literature, for instance. We might describe them as good readers or good critics. They do not expect to find anything in what they read for their edification. There is, however, another way of missing the point. There are people who read the story of Abraham not as a story of faith, but as a story of resignation, as a story of someone who has given up hope. And now they say that they have faith. They accept Abraham as a model but have missed the point of the model. Pretty clearly K. addresses his exposition to those who say that they have faith, and who know the story of Abraham, but who misunderstand it and who get their relationship to Abraham all wrong. They regard themselves as the children of Abraham. But they are rather like the children of Agamemnon or of Jephthah—who gave up what was required.

The heroes of resignation are in some outward respects like the hero of faith. How is it manifest that the hero of resignation is that and not a hero of faith? By the surroundings and by what he says. What makes the hero of faith is what lies in the background, namely, the promise. He is also called the hero of promise. He believed in the promise.

What to Abraham is the command to sacrifice—to do such and such things—is to God *a test of faith*, a stretching of the tension of faith to the utmost, the ordeal. What is involved is the tenacity of his belief in the promise—and this is something between God and his maker. K. is interested in representing this incident as an ordeal. Hence the "fear and trembling." Also this becomes the model of the Christian life. A Christian is one to whom much is promised and who stakes all—sacrifices all—trembling in the presence of the promise and the demands laid upon one. Above I should have said, "A test of Abraham, *a test of friendship.*" The language: "You didn't believe me, did you?" A promise of love.

People are puzzled about the meaning of expressions, sentences, etc., because they are guided, *not by a mistaken theory of meaning, but by a picture.* (Here is a use of the word "picture.") What determines their expectations is a picture of the explanation, someone's saying, "This is a *w*," and now, when it comes to an explanation, *they want something like that.* Fortunately, with most words they can get this. "This is a horse." Sometimes they also want what one might better describe as an introduction. "This is Dolly." Even that explanation of Dolly, "Who is Dolly?" may be made to puzzle them. Let us suppose that they begin saying that the world is made of particulars. They then need a name for particulars, and now, obviously, the explanation of Dolly won't suit them. If you were properly severe in these matters, you would realize that the Dolly today is not the Dolly tomorrow. Perhaps particulars are momentary and fleeting. So you need a new Dolly every minute. This puzzled Hume and he tried to figure this out. But if we suppose that the puzzle is not deepened in this way, then we may find that only certain expressions and their use puzzle us. "I" is such a word. And so are the psychological verbs. And: What is a cause?

Now then there must be certain expressions in the Scriptures which are like this. Chief among these is the word "God." And there must be many intelligent—they must be intelligent—and devout people who, though they pray and read the Scriptures with a reverent attitude and wince at blasphemy and at taking God's name in vain, yet are troubled at the question, Who is God? or, What is God? And what in this case troubles them? They are certainly groping for an explanation on the model of such explanations as they are familiar with. For what people want in such cases is not anything like, "God is the deity." It is curious in this connection that everybody—in a way—understands this word; atheists who say, "There is no God,"—which also shows how they are understanding this word; agnostics, who perhaps shrug their shoulders as though it were a matter of indifference and say, Who knows?; and believers to whom this is a matter of concern. The important thing in all these cases is to explore further the context of this sometimes militant denial, the indifference, and the assertion—that is, the further contexts, what else these people say who say or shrug. For what else they say will show how they are thinking of God—since that is their thinking of God. To check on such "aberrations" it is necessary to remind oneself of the Scriptural use of the word "God," the role of that word in the Scriptures. There are in the Scriptures no explanations. There are no arguments. There are, at most, announcements. No one here says, "Show me." Or do such misunderstandings sometimes come in? Either one must allow that there is this one Scriptural use, or if one discovers variations, one must settle upon some one guiding conception of which these variations are fringe. In any case the sorts of philosophical questions which we are concerned with arise within the community familiar with the Scriptures and are to be dealt with by reference to the Scriptures. This is not arbitrary. It is involved in the idea of the Christian religion. If the question arises among Mohammedans the same sorts of difficulties must give way to the words of the Koran. There are the Jewish, the Mohammedan, the Christian conceptions. The conception of "the fool who sayeth in his heart" is present in all three. And there may be a great deal of overlapping in what we may come to regard as the lesser essentials in each.

Consider: Spinoza's goings-on with the word "God."

Consider: Tillich's ground of all Being.

These are nonscriptural conceptions going about saying, "I'm God." They are in a Jewish or Christian community "impostors." Where, for instance, did Tillich get this idea? He intends this as a definition. But how is one to tell whether it is a correct definition? Can one substitute this expression in the Scriptures for the word "God"? Even if we run the word together "Groundofallbeing," it doesn't seem to do what the word "God" does. "In the beginning" what did the Groundofallbeing do? Did it create? What can grounds do?

Question: How do we use the word "God"?

Are not the Scriptures to teach us how to use it, learning our language from them? And their theology as the grammar. Also useful?

I have been saying that the language of Scripture is *the* language. And it is the model. Only by way of it do we learn to speak. But there is certainly something else. There is the language of the devout man in 1963. There is also the language of, let us say, Samuel Johnson in 17—. If you want, not so much to see what it is like, but to get a closer look at it, that is readily available. This has an added advantage, I think, since the language of Samuel Johnson is not the official language of the bishop, but that of a man who speaks and prays, not in an official capacity, but in great earnest, out of the trials and tribulations of his own life, his griefs, his temptations, his anguish, etc. With passion. That latter is important. It would perhaps be even more profitable if we had the language of some devout men now living, some we are now familiar with.

Saint Augustine's language would also be helpful.

And how now is one to study this? An aesthetic enquiry aimed at getting the feel of the language. For this, contrasts and comparisons are necessary. And what now would this be like? Consider the anguished language of either Saint Augustine or of Samuel Johnson in one of the great crises of his life, illness or death or temptation or something as ordinary as the view of the heavens or the sea ("seen as a creation filling one with wonder and fear," "the heavens declare. . . . the firmament showeth. . . ."). But now to get the hang of this one must contrast this with the language of unbelievers in comparable situations. For "all flesh is grass" and subject to the evils and sufferings, disappointments and successes, of other men.

The language of believers.

The language of man without God and without hope in the world. (Camus's Clamence.) (Dostoevsky's Writer of *The Notes.*)

This will, of course, get to be extremely complicated. The man, at any rate, who can speak is a man who cannot escape judging himself. ("hath not left man without witness—O, Man.") At any rate, it is the language of such men which is of interest to us.

There is also the language of men like Ivan and Clamence, who are brought up among believers and who spend a good part of their lives reacting to those believers and to what they say. Emptiness, meaninglessness, etc. Their lives are unintelligible apart from this reaction. They are rejectors and spend their thinking in active rejection and in defense. They flirt. They keep out but are, as it were, drawn to the outside of the ring, drawn and repelled. They want to enter but not by obedience and submission or by swooning. They are from Missouri, and want to be shown first. Intellectuals. Their terms cannot be met. So they stay out and live in "a waste and barren land." What I had in mind to ask, however, was something else: Their language is on the fringe—philosophical, perhaps—but also religious?

In connection with "religious" language there is a problem. What is it? If you regard Ivan as involved in a philosophical quandary, what is it? Consider the problem of evil. Is that, too, a philosophical problem? (a good subject) Ivan, Job—and Abraham, too? "Why should these terrible things happen?" (Ivan.) "Why should these things happen to *me?*" (Job.) Can we say that Ivan gets an answer? An illness and madness? Phenomena of guilt. If one were persuaded that evil in the world is "explained—and what would explanation here mean?—by recognition of one's own guilt would this now be shown in one's own humiliation?

"Why should these things happen?" This sounds as though we knew how it is that other things happen—and how is that?

"How is evil possible?" has the typical philosophical form. "How is science possible?"

The sort of problem? You make an engine according to a certain design. It should work perfectly. But then it doesn't. There are, as they say, bugs in it. And now they work to eliminate the bugs. They ask, Why doesn't it work as planned and expected? They find out, repair or replace a part, and then it works fine.

So too: God made a world, the best of all possible worlds, a world planned and designed to be a home, well furnished with all modern conveniences, or should I say a world in which conveniences are unnecessary, for man, designed for comfort and peace and prosperity with very little work, no sweat, no blood, no tears. There are people in this home, and they know the design. But now, instead of comfort and peace and prosperity with very little work, they find instead sweat ("In the sweat of thy brow") and blood (anger and murder) and tears (death and bereavement). They are naturally puzzled and greatly discomfited. At first they ask, "What went wrong?" There certainly are bugs in this world. Easily repaired? Much too big a job for our trouble-shooters. They discover that for sweat there are sweat glands, that anger is adrenaline and murder takes a muscle, and as for tears, they gather in the eyes and run down the cheeks. The evils seem to them to be built in. So in the end the more they know of the home and the inhabitants and the bugs, the less they believe in that story about the world, the golden age without bugs. God's bugs.

If I am to say that this, too, is a linguistic problem, the question then is as to how the religious, devout man reads the Creation story. Certainly it is not to be tested. It is not a theory or a hypothesis. *It provides man with a definite and limiting past.* It gives him a perspective, a framework for his life.

The Garden of Eden is a shambles. A boundary. Man needs boundaries.

Who are you?

Nothing's child. A bubble's baby. A foundling lost among the stones.

Religious language, Biblical language involves such questions as to how the Creation story is to be read. Myth? But how then is myth to be read? As we read Greek myth, Socrates gave us some direction for that: "I do not say . . . but something of the sort is true." (The myth of Judgment.) What if you believe the myth, what then? Is something to follow?

Who are these people who are so eager for proofs? After all these centuries and with all the ruins of proofs fallen around about us they still want proofs. They say that they want these proofs, not for themselves, but for others. But if they came to where they are, let us call it "faith," by some other way ("No man cometh unto the Father but by me"), then what makes them think that there is another way still to be invented by some clever believer, especially designed for clever unbelievers? Is the proof to serve in the stead of "a voice crying in the wilderness?" I have an idea that proofs are provoked among intellectuals (who else could design a proof?), by other intellectuals among whom are some who say, "I am an atheist since I see no good reason for believing that God exists." So the designing of a proof is a response to a challenge: "Prove it." The challenge itself is the expression of a confusion, since insofar as this arises in the context of Christianity, which is a gospel, proof is precisely what is ruled out. And if the challenge is the expression of a confusion, so too is the response. Revelation is not geometry. Neither is God on trial in a court of laws. There is neither proof nor evidence. But this does not mean that anything is lacking. You might as well complain that no one has proved, as yet, not only that the angels did sing, but the song itself. Prove "Glory to God in the highest."

People say that this is the infallible word (Which Word? Syllables or a Person?) And then they proceed to prove the Infallible Word by a word more infallible still. They are clever. And, by the way, if we say that this word is infallible how are we to understand that? Presumably it is a word that cannot fail. But cannot fail to do what? Is the word supposed to do something? What?

"Very intelligent and educated people believe in the story of Creation in the Bible, while others hold it to be patently false, and the grounds of the latter are well-known to the former."[1]

THE BIBLICAL PICTURE OF HUMAN LIFE

Here is the sentence that gave rise to difficulties: "It may be understood as a picture, a representation of our lives, a way of coming not only to understand ourselves, but a representation of a world in which a man may make his home." Let me see whether I can figure this out. "It may be understood as a picture." I might have said, "It may be understood as a story." What I wrote might then be regarded as a sketch of the picture

1. Ludwig Wittgenstein, *On Certainty*, ed. G. E. M. Anscombe and G. H. vonWright, trans. Denis Paul and G. E. M. Anscombe (New York: Harper and Row, 1969), p. 43.

or an outline of the story, and where now is that picture or that story? In the Bible, of course. If this sounds strange to you, remember that the first verse in Genesis is, "In the beginning . . . ," and this is something like, "Once upon a time . . . ," and remember, too, that the end of the story is a triumph over death, the chapter called "The Resurrection Story." As in the case of early novels, there is a great deal of commentary, explanations of the significance of the story, episodes, celebration poetry, drama, etc., something corresponding to the role of the chorus in a Greek play. Now, I don't suppose you will deny that there is this story. You may prefer the word "story" to the word "picture," though this may not be the main source of the difficulty.

I'll try now to show you why this bothers you. You may think that I said "and so it's just a picture," but I said little about the role of that picture in people's lives, though I did say a little. Notice now that there are many readers of that story and many different readings of it. There are people who enjoy reading the Bible as pure phantasy. There are all sorts of ways of being impressed. One might say that it is vastly superior to Homer. Of course, one may be aware that once upon a time, among primitive peoples, such stories were believed. But as is the case with children, they were not used to distinguishing between what they remembered and what they imagined. Accordingly, books like those interest people who are interested in folklore and in the fragments of history that such lore carried along with it. Other people are attached to the Bible as "the book of my people," and it won't matter now that I do not believe any of this. "My grandfather and the father of all my fathers is in this book." Many an unbelieving Jew must cherish at least a good part of this book. "My people." There is history, folklore, drama, story, poetry, morals, argument, parables, sermons, etc. Now I want to introduce a distinction. There are people who believe that this story is a story about themselves. "In the beginning God created me." You might be inclined to say that such people are afflicted with belief—for it isn't, or isn't necessarily, that such people are now cozy in their belief. Such belief may rather involve them in something more like a life of perpetual shock. They say that life with a genius is very difficult. His standards are much too high and are the source of misery not only to himself but also to those around about him. Consider then how it must be for any man who by the avenue of his belief, a sort of introduction, must for all the rest of his life put up with God as a daily companion. "His eye is on the sparrow." That may be well for the sparrow. But "His eye is on me"—what about that? "He knoweth our frame, that we are dust," "he knoweth the secrets of the heart," "he knew what is in the mind of man." *It's as though a man stepped into or was drawn into the picture or the story, and now everything in the picture came alive for him and he began a new life in that picture.* Pleasant! I have already suggested that it might be dreadful. "It is an awful thing to fall into the hands of. . . ." It must be a mistake to regard belief as a ticket to a picnic, and an everlasting picnic at that. I want now to return to the idea of the picture. What I have called the picture is the same for all. Now notice once more that some, perhaps nearly all, who are acquainted with the picture, stand before the picture, at ease admiring it, or stand gazing upon the picture, uncomfortably. Some do not pay any attention to the picture. They pass by and may even be repelled by it. And so on. The picture is there, for all. And now, I think, the language I used above may help us to see the difference. Some men, I said, are drawn into the picture, and everything in the picture now becomes alive for them, and with this their lives are changed, a new environment, a new life. But for others it is and remains just a picture. Nothing is changed. Life goes on and death takes all. The best player of all.

So much for clearing up what may have been misleading in the use of the word "picture." Now I want to pass on to a related difficulty.

I wrote, "And now if you ask, 'Is it true?' then I want to say that in the ordinary way in which this question is understood, it is neither true nor false." I want to consider this. Let me ask first, who are you who asks this question? If you are one of those—"We happy few;" or "of all men most miserable"—who have been drawn into the picture, then, of course, you will not ask. I said that everything has come alive for him. So the question now looks a little like, "Is it alive?" and this is rather like, "Am I alive?" since I am in the picture. Of course, we should no longer speak of *the picture.* What are called "living pictures" are people posing, and that is not what we want. So the question must be asked by someone who stands before the picture or who has just heard the story, by someone who is not in the picture. To the person not in the picture the picture is just a picture but to the person *in* the picture the picture is no longer a picture. It's a new world, "a new heaven and a new earth." So he who asks is not in the picture. And who then does he ask? Let's suppose he asks someone who is also not in the picture. Now it is obvious that this person is as incompetent to answer as he is himself. And it won't matter that this person says either "yes" or "no." Here, no investigation can be made. It isn't as though one could make his way around the picture to see whether there is something behind it. If you look behind the picture in this case, you'll find nothing behind it. So whoever asks will have to ask someone who has been drawn into the picture. And now will that help? Suppose he now answers, "How true," or "The still waters were never more still, the pastures never greener, and as for the valley of the shadow of death, I fear no evil," and so on, the outsider will surely make nothing of this. Certainly, a man who walks into a picture and begins talking to other figures in the picture and now sets up housekeeping in that frame, having found a home, is not exactly to be trusted. Ordinary batty people one may get on with, but there are limits.

The distinction between the man who stands before the picture and the man who is drawn into the picture and for whom all these things in the picture are now alive and whose life is renewed, corresponds to a distinction with which Kierkegaard is continually occupied. It is the distinction between (1) the man who is in various ways occupied with Christianity as a doctrine or a teaching—the picture—and who now wants to prove that it is true, or at least a little bit or a great deal true, and (2) the man who lives and suffers in the presence of the Most High, the man who is caught up in the picture. A Christian is one who is drawn into the picture. But a man may live under the illusion that he is a Christian just because he is so occupied and, perhaps favorably, with that picture. As we have seen, there are ever so many ways of being occupied.

There is one further matter in connection with that picture that occurred to me. In the center of that picture is the figure of a man. Let that represent a man's life. It is obvious that if the picture is to be complete, the surrounding spaces must be filled in. Man, after all, lives in surroundings, a good part of the surroundings we are familiar with. But in the picture that we are given in this case, there are details that no man could possibly have been acquainted with. Man's life, as we know it, once we are given the picture, is like a part of a picture torn out of the whole picture. Given such a part, it is obvious that artists might go about providing surroundings for that part (or fragment) in ever so many ways. Socrates, by the way, supplied such surroundings, surroundings that he regarded as involved somehow in details of the fragment, like railroad tracks leading away into the distance. I think that Kierkegaard regarded it as the glory of Socrates, not that he completed the picture, but that once having completed the picture as *the* picture, he stepped into it and never stepped out again. When other men said, "We'll kill you if you don't step out of that picture," he did not budge. (Neither did he live by bread alone.) Now notice that we can figure out pretty well how Socrates came to have just this picture. He needed this picture to explain the slave boy, or any other boy. But the picture that we are busy about, what about that? Apparently this picture no man ever made. God made it and he put himself into the picture, too. In fact, it was precisely in this way that he was to draw men into the picture.

(Curiously this idea of the picture has been surprisingly fertile.)

This suggests something concerning philosophy. From the little we know, or from some part of the little we know, we seek to extend our knowledge. What we know cannot be the whole picture, and one might say that we need the whole picture in order to understand the little we know. But where would one ever get the idea of the whole picture? Perhaps from religion. (This would not have come from mathematics—geometry.) This shows up in Socrates's interest in myth. It seems that this world and our lives in it have surroundings which do not show up in this world. Slender threads leading out. What threads? If we begin with what we know and seek to extend it—what would this be but science? What then? Better begin with confusion in the guise of knowledge—that leads us on to further confusion in the guise of knowledge.

God, the unknown—how then could a man fill out the picture?

Above I said that a man was drawn into the picture—but how? I added now "as by a magnet." ("And if I be lifted up I will draw all men unto me.") This way of putting it may help to make it clear that one does not climb into the picture, or step into it, by means of reasons or arguments, as though he understood something better than other men do.

When a man says it, let us say that he says it because it is true. And this involves that he found it out. But when God says it, God does not say it because it is true, as though God, too, had to find it out. When God says it, God ordains it, orders it. It is rather like, "Let there be light." God, remember, makes no mistakes. This parallels another remark. God does not ordain this because it is good, but it is good because God ordains it.

These things are said to remind us of what is and is not said. If I say that God makes no mistakes, I do not mean that God is more careful and more thorough in his research than nearly everybody.

Let us keep the problem as simple as we can. So let us not ask, What is Christianity? Let each one of us ask a different question. Let each of us ask a question that he might have some resources for answering. Let every Roman Catholic ask, What is Roman Catholicism? Or what does it mean to be a Roman Catholic? And if there is a Baptist here, let him ask the corresponding question. So too let any Presbyterian, Methodist, Episcopalian, and so on. If anyone should have difficulty answering his question, he will know where to go for the answer. Any Roman Catholic priest will be glad to enlighten anyone who asks him. And surely there must be someone to answer for anyone else. You need only ask and then listen. And with such an answer anyone must be satisfied since he will now be enlightened concerning what he is and has been all along.

No doubt anyone who is not any one of these—not having been brought up so—if he heard all these answers, would be bewildered. His bewilderment might be expressed in the question *But what then is Christianity?* since all these people say that they are Christians. And it might be supposed that someone would know. Well, I am that someone. All these—Roman Catholicism, Presbyterianism, Lutheranism, etc.— are forms of Christianity, and apart from these and as many forms as there are, there is no Christianity. It comes about in this way: There is a certain book, the Christian book called the Christian book because it is about one Jesus Christ who, according to the book, was before the world was made. This book has been terribly important to many people. There was a time when there were what may be called official readers of that book. They were appointed to tell anyone what was in that book. The time came, however, when the official readers no longer agreed on what the book said. First one disagreed with the one, then a third disagreed with the two, and then a fourth disagreed with the three, and so on. Each took it upon himself to tell the world what the book said and each had his listeners. And so it is we have Catholics, Lutherans, Presbyterians, and so on, all of whom are Christians since they do all read diligently the Christian book. So it happens that in 1966 if someone asks, What is Christianity? one may get as many answers as there are people one asked. The moral seems to be, If you don't know, don't ask, or ask but once.